TEACHER'S RESOURCE MANUAL
WITH PRINTMASTERS
PROJECT ACHIEVEMENT:

Reading

George D. Spache, Ph.D.
Spache Educational Consultants

Evelyn B. Spache, Ed.D.
Spache Educational Consultants

And the Scholastic Editors

Scholastic

PROJECT ACHIEVEMENT: *READING*

Teacher's Resource Manual With Printmasters

Curriculum Consultant:
Leonore K. Itzkowitz, Reading Specialist,
New Jersey Public School

Editorial Director:
Eleanor Angeles

Contributing Writers:
Meisha Goldish, Mary Ann Pomerleau,
Alexander Sinclair, Suzanne Sayegh Thomas

Editorial Supervision, Production, and Design:
ZIGG-LYN Publishing Concepts and Services,
Harry Chester Associates

ISBN 0-590-34718-7

12 11 10 9 8 7 6   0/9 1 2 3 4 5/9

Printed in the U.S.A.

CONTENTS

PROJECT ACHIEVEMENT: *READING* Book F

INTRODUCTION

Project Achievement: Reading is a series of books designed to help students become better readers and, ultimately, better test-takers. Each 224-page book provides instruction and practice in those reading skills that can be most easily transferred to the taking of achievement tests.

The skills in each book are organized into four units: **Reading Comprehension, Vocabulary, Study Skills,** and **Tests.** Each of the first three units contains individual lessons focusing on a particular skill. The instruction and practice in each lesson is developed around a nonfiction selection that is both interesting and within the ability range of your students.

Each book contains instruction and self-checking practice to help students develop strategies for dealing with the reading selections and activities, and the tests that follow. After the self-checking lessons have been completed, students may work independently on the lessons in the rest of the unit. However, teacher-directed lessons may result in more efficient mastery of the reading skills.

Within each unit are lessons on test-taking which are intended to reinforce students' understanding of the skills previously taught.

The specific reading skills being focused on in all the units are listed in the Scope and Sequence chart on pages 7-8 of this Teacher's Resource Manual.

At the end of this manual are printmasters intended for pretesting and reteaching of the skills covered in the student book.

There are also printmaster sheets for students:
- to record their answers to the question items in each unit of their book
- to fill out for writing about a selection just read
- to fill out when reading a related article in a newspaper or a magazine

To use these printmasters, make multiple copies of the test you need for preteaching or reteaching a specific skill. Distribute the copies to your students and have them write independently to complete the test.

PLACING STUDENTS IN THE PROGRAM

Books A-H of *Project Achievement: Reading* may be used with students at different levels of reading ability. The program is recommended primarily for students in middle schools and high schools who are reading at second-to tenth-grade levels.

The following charts show the ranges in ability level and interest level for users of Books A-H.

ABILITY LEVEL

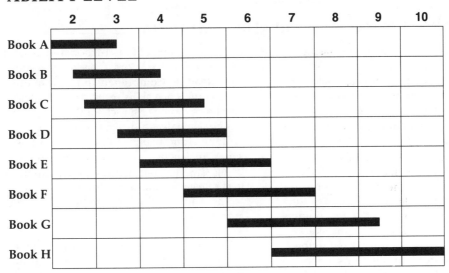

INTEREST LEVEL

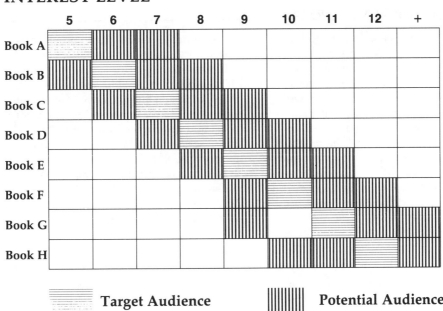

Target Audience   Potential Audience

FLEXIBLE PROGRAM FOR DIFFERENT ABILITY LEVELS

Project Achievement: Reading may be used in different ways, depending on the reading abilities of your students. For students who are functioning substantially below grade level, the series may be used for developmental, teacher-directed instruction in reading comprehension, vocabulary, study skills, and test-taking. For students who are reading one to three years below grade level, the books may provide remedial, independent activities with minimal teacher direction.

INFORMATIVE, HIGH QUALITY READING MATERIAL

Special care has been taken in the selection of reading materials for *Project Achievement: Reading*. The major criteria for each selection were its substance and interest level. While sentences have been structured for easy comprehension, no sacrifice in completeness or clarity of the material has been made for the sake of conforming to a readability formula.

   Project Achievement: Reading proves that easy-to-read stories can be highly interesting as well as informative. Each selection in this series retains its substance while remaining easy to understand. In addition, the skills which some critics claim are ignored in the teaching of easy-reading selections are the very skills that *Project Achievement: Reading* stresses most. For example, numerous studies show that students with reading problems are in particular need of instruction and practice in making inferences from a reading selection. In each **Reading Comprehension Unit** in this series, inference skills receive the greatest emphasis. Some critics claim that easy-to-read materials neglect to teach the vocabulary skill of finding and using context clues. In this series, instruction and practice in finding and using specific context clues are an important part of each **Vocabulary Unit.**

   The reading selections are listed by content area in the guide on pages 9-11 of this Teacher's Manual.

   The reading selections and skills in *Project Achievement: Reading* prove that easy-reading materials can be a valuable tool in helping students improve their reading ability.

SERIOUS, CONSISTENT FORMAT

Special consideration has been given to the physical design of *Project Achievement: Reading*. Most remedial readers use a large type size with wide spaces between the lines. However, this is not the style students are confronted with on achievement tests. Since a major purpose of this series is to prepare students for achievement tests, the design of the program has been purposefully selected to reflect that. The books use a standard-sized type. The answer sheets provided for students to record test answers simulate the answer sheets used on actual achievement tests.

   The textbooklike appearance of this series will encourage the use of the program as a serious preparation for the taking of achievement tests.

   The skills being taught, as well as the physical design and the answer sheet format are integral to the entire series. The same skill is being taught in the same page of each book in the series. (The skill level, however, varies for every book.) This consistency of design and format permits the teacher to use the different levels of the *Project Achievement: Reading* series conveniently with students of varying ability in any one class.

FLEXIBILITY

Project Achievement: Reading texts are written on different reading levels, but skills content is the same. This means that you can focus on your class's needs . . . whether you use all the books together to accommodate varying abilities . . . use them in sequence as students' scores improve . . . or choose specific content areas from the texts for a curriculum-related unit. Whatever you do, your Teacher's Manual is filled with creative ideas to help you get the most out of a program that means just what the title says: *Achievement!*

Book

READING COMPREHENSION SKILLS	A	B	C	D	E	F	G	H
Details	(pp. 8-27)	(pp. 8-27)	(pp. 8-27)	(pp. 8-29)	(pp. 8-29)	(pp. 8-29)	(pp. 8-29)	(pp. 8-29)
Recognizing significant facts	✔	✔	✔	✔	✔	✔	✔	✔
Identifying a sequence	✔	✔	✔	✔	✔			
Identifying cause and effect	✔	✔	✔	✔	✔	✔	✔	✔
Recognizing the language of detail questions	✔	✔	✔	✔	✔	✔	✔	✔
Taking Tests	✔	✔	✔	✔	✔	✔	✔	✔
Main Idea	(pp. 28-49)	(pp. 28-49)	(pp. 28-49)	(pp. 8-29)	(pp. 8-29)	(pp. 8-29)	(pp. 8-29)	(pp. 8-29)
Finding a main idea for an entire selection	✔	✔	✔	✔	✔	✔		
Finding a main idea for part of a selection	✔	✔	✔					
Recognizing an appropriate title	✔	✔	✔	✔	✔	✔	✔	✔
Recognizing the language of main-idea questions	✔	✔	✔	✔	✔	✔	✔	✔
Taking Tests	✔	✔	✔	✔	✔	✔	✔	✔
Inference	(pp. 50-78)	(pp. 50-78)	(pp. 50-78)	(pp. 30-59)	(pp. 30-59)	(pp. 30-59)	(pp. 30-59)	(pp. 30-59)
Drawing a conclusion	✔	✔	✔	✔	✔	✔	✔	✔
Identifying character traits	✔	✔	✔	✔	✔	✔	✔	✔
Predicting outcomes		✔	✔	✔	✔	✔	✔	✔
Inferring cause and effect	✔	✔	✔	✔	✔	✔	✔	✔
Interpreting figurative language	✔	✔	✔	✔	✔	✔	✔	✔
Recognizing the language of inference questions	✔	✔	✔	✔	✔	✔	✔	✔
Taking Tests	✔	✔	✔	✔	✔	✔	✔	✔
Critical Reading				(pp. 60-78)	(pp. 60-78)	(pp. 60-78)	(pp. 60-78)	(pp. 60-78)
Determining the author's purpose				✔	✔	✔	✔	✔
Identifying opinion				✔	✔	✔	✔	✔
Identifying evidence for opinions				✔	✔	✔	✔	✔
Distinguishing fact from opinion				✔	✔	✔	✔	✔
Identifying the author's credentials				✔	✔	✔	✔	✔
Taking Tests				✔	✔	✔	✔	✔

Book

VOCABULARY SKILLS	A	B	C	D	E	F	G	H
Words and Meaning	(pp. 80-111)	(pp. 80-111)	(pp. 80-111)	(pp. 80-109)	(pp. 80-109)	(pp. 80-109)	(pp. 80-109)	(pp. 80-109)
Synonyms	✔	✔	✔	✔	✔	✔	✔	✔
Antonyms	✔	✔	✔	✔	✔	✔	✔	✔
Homonyms	✔	✔						
Taking Tests	✔	✔	✔	✔	✔	✔	✔	✔

VOCABULARY SKILLS (concluded)	A	B	C	D	E	F	G	H
Context Clues	(pp. 112-127)	(pp. 112-127)	(pp. 112-127)	(pp. 110-125)	(pp. 110-125)	(pp. 110-125)	(pp. 110-125)	(pp. 110-125)
Definition clue	✔	✔	✔	✔	✔	✔	✔	✔
Synonym clue	✔	✔	✔	✔	✔	✔	✔	✔
Antonym clue	✔	✔	✔	✔	✔	✔	✔	✔
Experience clue	✔	✔	✔	✔	✔	✔	✔	✔
Series clue		✔	✔	✔	✔	✔	✔	✔
Taking Tests	✔	✔	✔	✔	✔	✔	✔	✔
Words with Several Meanings	(pp. 128-139)	(pp. 128-139)	(pp. 128-139)	(pp. 126-137)	(pp. 126-137)	(pp. 126-137)	(pp. 126-137)	(pp. 126-137)
Multiple Meanings	✔	✔	✔	✔	✔	✔	✔	
Taking Tests	✔	✔	✔	✔	✔	✔	✔	
Word Structure	(pp. 140-148)	(pp. 140-148)	(pp. 140-148)	(pp. 138-146)	(pp. 138-146)	(pp. 138-146)		
Compound words	✔	✔	✔	✔	✔	✔	✔	✔
Base words/Affixes	✔	✔	✔	✔	✔	✔	✔	✔
Taking Tests	✔	✔	✔	✔	✔	✔	✔	✔

STUDY SKILLS	A	B	C	D	E	F	G	H
Using Visual Materials	(pp. 150-173)	(pp. 150-173)	(pp. 150-173)	(pp. 148-173)	(pp. 148-173)	(pp. 148-173)	(pp. 148-173)	(pp. 148-173)
Map Reading	✔	✔	✔	✔	✔	✔	✔	✔
Calendars	✔	✔						
Tables	✔	✔	✔	✔	✔	✔	✔	✔
Pictographs	✔	✔						
Bar Graphs	✔	✔	✔	✔	✔	✔	✔	✔
Line Graphs	✔	✔	✔	✔	✔	✔	✔	✔
Circle Graphs	✔	✔	✔	✔	✔	✔	✔	✔
Taking Tests	✔	✔	✔	✔	✔	✔	✔	✔
Using Reference Materials	(pp. 174-196)	(pp. 174-196)	(pp. 174-196)	(pp. 174-196)	(pp. 174-196)	(pp. 174-196)	(pp. 174-196)	(pp. 174-196)
Alphabetical Order	✔	✔	✔	✔	✔	✔	✔	✔
Dictionary	✔	✔	✔	✔	✔	✔	✔	✔
Table of Contents	✔	✔	✔	✔	✔	✔	✔	✔
Index	✔	✔	✔	✔	✔	✔	✔	✔
Card Catalog	✔	✔	✔	✔	✔	✔	✔	✔
Encyclopedia	✔	✔	✔	✔	✔	✔	✔	✔
Atlas				✔	✔	✔	✔	✔
Almanac	✔	✔	✔	✔	✔	✔	✔	✔
Newspapers & Magazines			✔	✔	✔	✔	✔	✔
Readers' Guide to Periodical Literature			✔	✔	✔	✔	✔	✔
Choosing the Right Source	✔	✔	✔	✔	✔	✔	✔	✔
Taking Tests	✔	✔	✔	✔	✔	✔	✔	✔

CONTENT CHART

CONTENT		BOOK D	BOOK E	BOOK F
SOCIAL STUDIES	**HISTORY**	"The Uniform Factory," p. 18 "The Birth of a Bridge," p. 52 "The Take-Off," p. 54 "Dollar Facts," p. 90 "Marathon Dancing," p. 114 A Balloon Flight, p. 125 "Black Cowboys, Yesterday and Today," p. 132 "Valley Forge," p. 152 "Then and Now," p. 158 "How Many Are We?" p. 168 "I'll Trade You," p. 178 "Ballooning," p. 186 "The Prize," p. 192	"Living in an Octagon," p. 14 "Looking for the Past," p. 22 Jenner Cures Smallpox, p. 57 Wrong Way Corrigan, p. 81 Leaning Tower of Pisa, p. 82 "The Sad Sound of Success," p. 86 "Navaho Code-Talkers," p. 88 Sinking of the Titanic, p. 97 "Japan Opens Its Doors," p. 118 Patent Laws, p. 125 "Fires in the Sky," p. 178 "Twice Is Enough," p. 184 The Old-Time Milkmen, p. 198 The Fishing Reel, p. 200 Machu Picchu, p. 211	"Farewell to Checkers," p. 12 "Saving a Symbol," p. 16 "The Treasure in the Cave," p. 18 "Remembering the Names," p. 22 Leaning Tower of Pisa, p. 28 "Cracking an Ancient 'Code'" p. 52 "The First President," p. 84 "Japanese Prison Camps in the United States," p. 90 "In Peace and War," p. 158 "Uncovering the Past," p. 184 Crossing the Delaware, p. 200
	GEOG-RAPHY	"Western Overgrowth," p. 144 "The Tip of Manhattan," p. 150 "Number One," p. 154 "Rain and Crops," p. 156 "The Water Planet," p. 166	"Snow Job," p. 12 "The Polar Bear Capital of the World," p. 34 "Arctic Adventure," p. 46 "An Iceberg in the Desert?" p. 98 Central America, p. 148 "Cape Cod," p. 150 "Thundering Waters," p. 152 "City on a Lake," p. 154	"Cracks on the Land," p. 14 Soviet Union, p. 29 "The Company town," p. 38 "Cities on the Rise," p. 98 "Reliving a Legend," p. 102 "Inner Space," p. 150 "The Terrific Tree of Tenerife," p. 154 "A Boom Is on the Way," p. 176 "Daybreak Debate," p. 192
	BIOG-GRAPHY	"Taking Command," p. 36 "Super Sculpture," p. 42 "How I Learned To High Jump," p. 74 Presidential Facts, pp. 81, 82, 96, 97 "The Perfect Secretary," p. 100 "A Young Business Leader," p. 102 "Dorothea Dix, Prison Reformer," p. 120 "A Matter of Age?" p. 188 Jim Thorpe, p. 214	"Getting Down to Business," p. 36 "Sculptor of Dreams," p. 50 "The Story of Kenny Washington," p. 54 "The Autograph Hound," p. 84 "A Black Leader for All People," p. 92 "A Great Sports Reporter," p. 102	"The Tree Inspector," p. 24 "It's a Snap," p. 54 "Good Tunes," p. 68 "New Life in a New Land," p. 100 "The Wise and Humble King," p. 120 "Connecting the Generations," p. 144 "Brooklyn Babies," p. 188

CONTENT CHART

ANALYSIS OF READING ACHIEVEMENT TESTS

One of the objectives of *Project Achievement: Reading* is to prepare students for reading achievement tests they will take during their school careers. To accomplish this aim, the content and design of the series were patterned after the content and design of standardized achievement tests.

Five major reading achievement tests were analyzed for their content and style: the Comprehensive Tests of Basic Skills (CTBS), the Stanford Achievement Tests, the Metropolitan Achievement Tests (MAT), the IOWA Tests of Basic Skills, and the California Achievement Tests (CAT).

The results of this analysis showed that most test items came under one of three strands: reading comprehension, vocabulary, and study skills. In the comprehension strand, students were required to identify details, determine the main idea, draw inferences, and determine a writer's purpose in a reading passage. In the vocabulary strand, students used synonyms, antonyms, homonyms, context clues, and word parts to determine the meaning of a word. In the study skills strand, students found information using visual and reference materials.

In addition to the study of achievement tests, an analysis was made of three state assessment programs: the New Jersey Minimum Basic Skills Testing Program, the Texas Assessment of Minimum Skills, and the California Assessment Program. The scope of these tests proved to be similar to that of the achievement tests studied.

The circle graphs on this page depict the scope of the sixth- and twelfth-grade assessments.

The skills content of *Project Achievement: Reading* reflects the content of the major achievement and assessment tests. In addition, the tests provided in this series follow the format of the standardized tests. Each test item is a multiple-choice question.

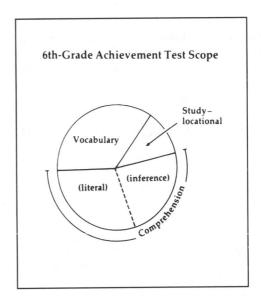

6th-Grade Achievement Test Scope

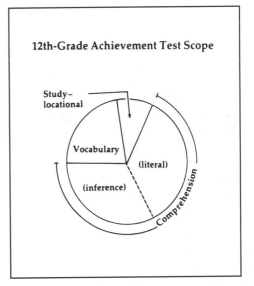

12th-Grade Achievement Test Scope

Wording of the directions includes such terms as *passage* and *selection*, which often appear on the achievement tests. The series also provides answer sheets that simulate the variety of styles found on standardized tests.

STRUCTURE OF THE PROGRAM

There are four units in *Project Achievement: Reading.* They are: (1) **Reading Comprehension**, (2) **Vocabulary**, (3) **Study Skills**, and (4) **Tests**. Below is an analysis of each of the four units. Starting on page 17 of this Teacher's Manual are teaching suggestions and answers for each of the lessons, exercises, and tests throughout the student text.

UNIT I □ READING COMPREHENSION

Unit Content

The **Reading Comprehension Unit** in each book consists of 27 lessons grouped in three parts. In Books A, B, and C there is (1) Details, (2) Main Idea, and (3) Inference. In Books D through G there is (1) Details and Main Idea, (2) Inference, and (3) Critical Reading. Each part provides instruction and practice in a major reading comprehension skill.

As each new skill is introduced, previous skills are reinforced. Questions in the *inference* part review the two previous skills taught—finding details and determining the main idea. Questions in the *critical reading* part review the skills of finding details, determining the main idea, and making inferences.

The selection of these particular skills reflect their importance in the reading comprehension portions of the most widely used achievement tests. Of the 27 lessons in the unit, more lessons focus on the skills of making inferences and critical reading than on the other reading skills. Numerous studies have shown that students with reading problems are particularly in need of instruction in making inferences and in critical reading.

Each part of the unit contains specific strategies to help students improve their ability to handle any reading materials, including those on comprehension tests. In addition, each part includes an introduction to the reading skill followed by two practice

lessons. Every question in the practice lessons gives an explanation of how the correct answer can be found. These suggested techniques for answering questions can then be applied in the lessons that follow. At the end of each part of the unit is a section on test-taking. These tests are modeled after achievement tests and are intended to reinforce students' understanding of the skills taught. The tests also recommend strategies, called **Test Tips,** for handling test questions, and give the students practice in following the directions they will encounter on standardized achievement tests.

About the Lessons

In each lesson, students read a nonfiction passage or poem and answer multiple-choice questions about the selection. These selections deal with a wide variety of subjects and include many themes that can be used to supplement several curriculum areas. (The chart on pages 9-11 groups the articles throughout the book according to content themes.)

The selections in the lessons, as well as the instructional materials and exercises, are written at the range of reading levels designated for this book (see chart on page 5). Specific suggestions for teaching the lessons and answers to the exercises appear on pages 17-65 of this Teacher's Manual.

UNIT II □ VOCABULARY

Unit Content

The **Vocabulary Unit** consists of 21 lessons grouped in four parts: (1) Synonyms and Antonyms, (2) Context Clues, (3) Words with Several Meanings, and (4) Word Parts. Each

part introduces a different strategy for understanding and explaining the meanings of new vocabulary words. In Part 1, students match new words with synonyms and antonyms to define the words. In Part 2, students look for specific clues in the reading context. In Part 3, they determine which of a word's multiple meanings fits a given context. In Part 4, students look for a clue to the meaning of a word within the structure of the new word itself. In addition, there are four Word Reviews designed so students may review new words from the lessons.

Emphasis throughout the **Vocabulary unit** is on the students' ability to recognize and select synonyms or antonyms for words. This emphasis matches the focus of most achievement tests that students will take during their school careers. Even in the *Context Clues* part of the unit (Part 2), emphasis is on recognition of synonyms or antonyms of new words in the reading selections. Recognizing context clues is an essential skill for taking achievement tests. Therefore, it is important that special attention be paid to recognizing and using these clues.

Each part of the unit begins with several pages of instruction and self-checking practice to help students develop the strategy for dealing with new words in the reading selections, activities, and tests that follow. Each part concludes with a section on test-taking to evaluate the students' understanding of the new words and to strengthen their ability to use vocabulary strategies. **Test Tips** on how to deal with vocabulary test questions are provided.

About the Lessons
In each lesson, students are introduced to eight or ten new vocabulary words at the top of each page. For the lessons in Part 1, the new words are explained by using simpler synonyms. For all other lessons, students use context clues to define the new words.

The new words in each lesson are highlighted in dark type in each nonfiction reading selection. The lessons follow a pattern. First, students focus on the look and sound of the new words. Then they read the words in context and reinforce their understanding through the activities. Finally, students use the words in their own sentences.

As in Unit I, the selections in the lessons are written at the range of reading levels designated for this book (see chart on page 5). The highlighted vocabulary words within each lesson, however, are two to four grade levels higher, because students reading below grade level are often tested on vocabulary several levels higher. Since the general level of each selection is within most students' reading capabilities, students can focus effectively on the more difficult vocabulary words. The new words generally fit with the theme of the reading selection, so the context can help students recognize and remember them. Most of the words are from the *Basic Reading Vocabularies* list compiled by Albert J. Harris and Milton D. Jacobson (Macmillan, 1982).

Specific suggestions for teaching the lessons and answers to the exercises appear on pages 17-65 of this Teacher's Manual.

About the Glossary
A three-page Glossary is presented at the end of the student book (pages 218-220). The Glossary contains all of the words presented in this unit, with the meaning(s) that apply in the reading selections.

Students can use the Glossary to check their answers or to review the words.

UNIT III □ STUDY SKILLS _____

Unit Content
The **Study Skills Unit** consists of 19 lessons in two parts: (1) Visual Materials and (2) Reference Skills. Each part provides instruction and practice in basic study skills. In Part 1, students find information by using visual materials including maps, tables, and graphs. In Part 2, students find information by using reference materials including a dictionary, an encyclopedia, an almanac, an atlas, a newspaper, a magazine, and the card catalog.

The skills in each part have been chosen

because of their importance in many achievement tests, and because of their value to many aspects of student work. Each part of the unit presents students with the necessary information and strategies to improve their competency in using visual or reference materials. Each part begins with an introduction to the specific study skills to be presented in the lessons. At the conclusion of each part is a section on test-taking to determine students' ability to use visual and reference materials. The test pages also provide several strategies, **Test Tips**, for improvement of test-taking skills.

About the Lessons

In each lesson, students are introduced to a new study skill involving the use of a visual or reference material. Each lesson begins with a motivational, nonfiction reading selection. The selection is accompanied by a graphic illustration based on information in the reading selection. This is followed by an explanation of the study skill and a series of multiple-choice questions about the material. The first question is always answered in the text and is followed by an explanation of the answer.

The 10 lessons in Part 1 introduce students to skills involving different types of maps, tables, and graphs. The nine lessons in Part 2 introduce skills involving the use of a dictionary, an encyclopedia, an almanac, an atlas, a newspaper, a magazine, and the card catalog. Although each lesson focuses on a new skill, many lessons reinforce and build upon previously taught skills.

The reading selections, along with instructional materials and exercises, are written at the range of reading levels designated for this book (see chart on page 5). Formal terms such as *compass rose* and *coordinates* are used in the lessons when they apply to the skill.

Specific suggestions for teaching the lessons and answers to the exercises appear on pages 17-65 of this Teacher's Manual.

UNIT IV ☐ TESTS

How To Use the Tests

Several tests are provided in this book for the **Reading Comprehension, Vocabulary,** and **Study Skills Units.** Tests within a unit come at the end of every part in each unit. In addition, the last unit consists of two cumulative tests.

The tests in *Project Achievement: Reading* follow the format used by many of the standardized achievement tests. Each test item is a multiple-choice question with four answer choices, only one of which is correct. The wording in the test directions and test items is like that often found on achievement tests. Terms such as *selection, passage, article,* and *item* are used.

Tests Within the Units

The tests in the **Reading Comprehension Unit** require students to identify details and main ideas, make inferences, and apply critical reading skills to answer questions about a passage. The tests in the **Vocabulary Unit** require students to determine the meaning of words through the use of synonyms, antonyms, context clues, multiple-meaning definitions, and word parts. The tests in the **Study Skills Unit** require students to find information using visual materials (maps, tables, graphs) and reference materials (dictionary, encyclopedia, almanac, atlas, etc.).

The tests that conclude each part of a unit serve a dual purpose. First, they measure students' understanding of the skills taught in that part of the unit. (Tests in the **Vocabulary Unit** review the words taught in that unit.) Second, they will provide several test-taking strategies, called **Test Tips.** The test tips are different for each test. Many of the test tips can be applied to other tests in the unit and to test-taking in general. Students record their answers on answer sheets similar in format to those on actual achievement tests. The answer sheets are located on pages 83-96 in this Teacher's Manual. They may be reproduced or copied.

End-of-the-Book Tests

The two cumulative tests at the end of the book test all the skills taught in the units. Each test has three sections: **Reading Comprehension, Vocabulary,** and **Study Skills.** Test directions in the cumulative tests are worded like the directions on the major achievement tests in order to give students more experience with achievement tests situations. Therefore, no test tips are presented in the cumulative tests. Students record their answers on answer sheets similar to those used on actual achievement tests. The answer sheets are located on pages 83-96 of this Teacher's Manual. They may be reproduced for each unit.

Time Limits for Testing

No time limits have been set for the tests in the book. Setting a time restriction, either for tests within each unit or for the cumulative tests in Unit IV, is optional. However, since a major purpose of the program is to prepare students for timed achievement tests, you may find it valuable to impose a time limit on tests. A suggested guideline for timing cumulative tests is found on page 65 of this Teacher's Manual.

Books

Beech, John R. *Learning to Read, A Cognitive Approach to Reading and Poor Reading.* San Diego, California: College Hall Press, 1985.

Dale, Edgar, and O'Rourke, Joseph. *The Living Word Vocabulary.* Chicago: World Book—Childcraft International, 1981.

Dale, Edgar, and O'Rourke, Joseph. *Techniques of Teaching Vocabulary.* Menlo Park, California: The Benjamin/Cummings Publishing Company, 1971.

Feder, Bernard. *The Complete Guide to Taking Tests.* Englewood Cliffs, N.J.: Prentice-Hall, Inc., 1979.

Guszak, Frank J. *Reading Instruction in the Elementary School.* 3rd ed. New York: Harper & Row, 1985.

Harris, Albert J., and Jacobson, Milton D. *Basic Reading Vocabularies.* New York: Macmillan Publishing Co., Inc., 1982.

Spache, Evelyn B. *Reading Activities for Child Involvement.* Boston: Allyn and Bacon, 1982.

Spache, George D., and Berg, Paul Conrad. *The Art of Efficient Reading.* 4th ed. New York: Macmillan Publishing Co. Inc., 1985.

Spache, George D. *Good Reading for Poor Readers.* Champaign, Ill.: Garrard Publishing Company, 1978.

Studies

Beck, Isabel L. et al. *Instructional Dimensions That May Affect Reading Comprehension: Examples from Two Commercial Reading Programs.* Learning Research and Development Center, University of Pittsburgh, 1979.

Hurwitz, David A. *Test Taking.* ED 169 109. Arlington, Va.: ERIC Document Reproduction Service, 1978.

Stewart, Oran, and Green, Dan S. "Test-Taking Skills for Standardized Tests of Reading." *The Reading Teacher.* March 1983, pp. 634-638.

Wilson, Lucy R. *Teaching Test-Taking Strategies.* ED 160 929. Arlington, Va.: ERIC Document Reproduction Service, 1977.

Teaching Suggestions and Answer Keys

INTRODUCTION TO THE BOOK (Pages 5-6)

Objectives
Students will:
■ be presented a sampling of the four units in the book: **Reading Comprehension, Vocabulary, Study Skills,** and **Tests.**
■ become acquainted with the kinds of reading selections and exercises they will be working with in the book.

Summary
Four different ways of improving reading and test-taking skills are presented. A passage about the 911 emergency telephone number and another about the first burglar-alarm system are followed by detail and main-idea questions and a vocabulary exercise. A chart showing the relationship between a nation's population and the number of phones in each is presented.

Teaching Suggestions
The benefits of these warm-up exercises may best be realized by asking students to complete them as an oral activity. Answers may be written afterward. Problems with handling the format for any of the four exercises can then be identified and corrected before students begin the actual lessons.

Answer Key
1. b; **2.** complex—complicated, identify—name, crucial—important, relays—transfers; **3.** Canada and the United States; **4.** d

UNIT I *Reading Comprehension*

PART 1 □ DETAILS AND MAIN IDEA

Introduction (Pages 8-9)

Objectives
Students will:
- focus on finding details and determining the main idea in a reading passage.
- understand reading selections at the literal level.

Summary of Lesson Material
Students are presented with a picture of people white-water rafting and a selection about previewing travel destinations using a computer.

Teaching Suggestions
The eight lessons in Part 1 provide instruction and practice in these skills. Students read the selection in each lesson and learn how to answer multiple-choice questions about details and how to use details to determine the main idea.

The photograph, passage, and exercise on pages 8-9 are a warm-up activity for finding details and the main idea in a reading selection. A brief discussion of the photograph will help to focus attention on the variety of details and the general idea of the photo. In the directions preceding the selection on page 9, call attention to the term *passage*. The term is commonly found on achievement tests. After students have read the passage and completed the exercise, review the answers together. Have volunteers identify the details in the passage that lead to correct answers for items 1 and 2. Then ask students to explain why answer choice **b** in item 3 is the best statement of the main idea. Emphasize that important details in the passage are clues to the main idea.

Answer Key
1. d, **2.** a, **3.** b

LESSON 1 □ Uninvited Guests (Pages 10-11)

Objectives
Students will:
- be introduced to the basic lesson format which is consistent throughout the **Reading Comprehension Unit.**
- be provided techniques for selecting the right answers to questions that require finding details or determining the main idea.

Summary of Lesson Material
Moose venture into Anchorage, Alaska when heavy snow prevents them from getting to their regular food sources.

Teaching Suggestions
These are self-checking exercises; the correct answer and an explanation for selecting that particular answer are given for each question.

In **Lesson 1,** encourage students to look back at the selection to locate the correct detail for each answer. To reinforce the skill of locating details, volunteers may read sentences from the passage with the correct detail for each answer. To reinforce the skill of locating details, volunteers may read from the passage with the correct details. As students practice this skill, they will gain experience in locating details quickly without rereading the entire selection. Make sure students understand that only one of the four answers choices in each item is correct. Encourage students to select an answer for each question before reading the explanation under **Check your answer.**

Answer Key
1. d, **2.** c, **3.** b, **4.** c

LESSON 2 ☐ Farewell to Checkers (Pages 12-13)

Objectives
Students will:
■ be provided techniques for selecting the right answers to questions that require finding details or determining the main idea.

Summary of Lesson Material
Checker cabs lost their taxi market share because they used too much gas. To create a new design would have proved too costly. Therefore, the Checker Motor Company stopped production in the early 1980's.

Teaching Suggestions
The format of **Lesson 2** is different from that of **Lesson 1.** Answers and explanations are grouped at the end of all the questions, rather than after each one. Students may test themselves by first answering all the questions and then checking the answers afterward.

Students who selected wrong answers should be encouraged to read the appropriate explanation in the **Check your answer** section to find the right details in the passage. Items 1-3 require a knowledge of details in the passage; item 4 is a main-idea question. Encourage students to pay close attention to the wording of the questions in the practice lessons. Similar wording is used in the other lessons in the **Reading Comprehension Unit,** as well as on the major achievement tests. One example is the phrase "This passage is mainly about _____" (item 4) to designate a question about the main idea of a passage. In addition, each question is either a complete sentence or a sentence completion, so that students will become familiar with both formats.

Answer Key
1. b, **2.** b, **3.** a, **4.** d

LESSON 3 ☐ Cracks in the Land (Pages 14-15)

Objectives
Students will:
■ be provided techniques for selecting the right answers to questions that require finding details or determining the main idea.

Summary of Lesson Material
Cracks that are hundreds of feet long and up to five feet deep are appearing in Arizona because underground water is being pumped to supply the needs of the increasing population there.

Teaching Suggestions
The **Check your answer** feature does not appear in **Lessons 3-8.** Although students may work independently on these lessons, teacher-directed lessons may result in more effective use of this material. Discuss each reading selection with the students before they answer the questions. Students' answers should be checked soon after they are completed for immediate reinforcement.

    Lesson 3 includes five questions about details in the reading passage and one (item 2) about its main idea. Point out that the answer choice "All of the above" in item 3 is sometimes used on achievement tests. While that is the correct answer for this item, it may be an incorrect choice on other items. Item 5 asks about a detail that is *not* mentioned in the passage. Encourage students to watch for key words like *not* that could change the meaning of a question.

Answer Key
1. c, **2.** d, **3.** d, **4.** c, **5.** a, **6.** b

LESSON 4 □ Saving a Symbol (Pages 16-17)

Objectives
Students will:
■ be provided techniques for and practice in selecting the right answers to questions that require finding details or determining the main idea.

Summary of Lesson Material
The Statue of Liberty has been repaired for its one hundredth anniversary.

Teaching Suggestions
In **Lesson 4,** emphasize the importance of reading each item carefully. In item 5, for example, two answer choices, **c** and **d,** are worded similarly. A hasty reading of the item could lead to an incorrect answer choice. If students decide that the first three answer choices are incorrect, they should pick choice **d,** "The passage does not say." This choice is similar to "None of the above," a choice sometimes given on standardized tests.

Answer Key
1. a, **2.** c, **3.** d, **4.** b, **5.** c

LESSON 5 □ The Treasure in the Cave (Pages 18-19)

Objectives
Students will:
■ be provided techniques for and practice in selecting the right answers to questions that require finding details or determining the main idea.

Summary of Lesson Material
Indian drawings from four hundred to eight hundred years ago were discovered insides caves in Tennessee.

Teaching Suggestions
In **Lesson 5,** point out that sometimes the correct detail to answer an item is quoted directly from the passage, but at other times, the detail may be paraphrased. In item 1, the correct answer ("they are in good condition") is a paraphrase of the wording in the selection ("very well preserved").

Answer Key
1. c, **2.** c, **3.** d, **4.** c, **5.** b, **6.** a

LESSON 6 ☐ Japan Tunes In (Pages 20-21)

Objectives
Students will:
■ be provided with techniques for and practice in selecting the right answers to questions that require finding details or determining the main idea.

Summary of Lesson Material
In Japan, family life in the evening centers around television. The Japanese are the world's leading television watchers with 98% of the homes having color televisions.

Teaching Suggestions
In **Lesson 6,** item 1 requires that students use a detail in the passage, "98 percent," to choose the correct answer choice, "nearly all." Item 5 asks for a definition—a common kind of question on reading comprehension tests. Encourage students to look quickly through the passage to find the word and its meaning.

Answer Key
1. b, **2.** a, **3.** d, **4.** c, **5.** d, **6.** b

LESSON 7 ☐ Remembering the Names (Pages 22-23)

Objectives
Students will:
■ practice answering detail and main-idea questions.
■ will be presented forms of main idea questions.

Summary of Lesson Material
Maya Ying Lin's design was chosen for the Vietnam Veterans Memorial in Washington, D.C. which was completed in 1982.

Teaching Suggestions
In **Lesson 7,** point out the various forms that a main-idea question can have. (For example: "This passage is mainly about _____" or "Which of these best describes the main idea of the passage?") For item 5, explain that even though

the passage already has a title, another title may better express the main idea of the passage.

Answer Key
1. c, **2.** b, **3.** c, **4.** d, **5.** b, **6.** a

LESSON 8 □ The Tree Inspector (Pages 24-25)

Objectives
Students will:
- practice answering detail and main-idea questions.
- use math to answer detail questions.

Summary of Lesson Material
Glen Patterson is a tree inspector in Manhattan who tries to keep trees there healthy.

Teaching Suggestions
In **Lesson 8,** have a volunteer explain the mathematics involved in determining the correct answer to item 1. In this final lesson on details and main idea, students may read sentences from the passage with the correct details to reinforce the skill of locating details.

Answer Key
1. a, **2.** d, **3.** b, **4.** b, **5.** c, **6.** c

TAKING TESTS (Pages 26-29)

Objectives
Students will:
- review the reading skills covered in the previous eight lessons.
- familiarize themselves with the format of standardized tests as they complete four reading comprehension tests.

Summary of Test Material (Page 26)
Scientists in Florida have discovered that two kinds of spiders weave white bands in the centers of their webs to warn off birds.

Summary of Test Material (Page 27)
Known for their swiftness in the water and their haunting cries, the Loon is an unforgettable bird.

Summary of Test Material (Page 28)
The Leaning Tower of Pisa is sixteen feet off center because of changes in the pressure of the pool of water underneath it.

Summary of Test Material (Page 29)
The Soviet Union occupies one sixth of the earth's land surface and has many of its geographical features. This country borders the United States on the western shores of Alaska and is halfway around the world from the U.S.'s eastern coast.

Teaching Suggestions

There are four tests in this section, consisting of reading selections and multiple-choice questions. The format for these tests is patterned after the reading comprehension portion of the major achievement tests. Note that the fourth test (page 29) is a cloze test, in which students are required to supply the missing word in a passage from a group of four answer choices. The cloze format has been included because it is widely used to determine students' ability to comprehend reading selections.

The **Test Tips** are intended to help students improve their test-taking skills. There is a different test tip on each practice page, but all of the tips can be applied in any test-taking situation.

Before students begin the tests, read through the directions and **Test Tips** with them. Emphasize that each question has four answer choices and that only one choice is correct. If students are using answer sheets to record their answers (see pages 83-96 of this Manual), tell them to fill in the space on the answer sheet that goes with the letter of the answer they choose. Caution students to make their marks dark and to fill in the space completely. To change an answer, students must erase the old mark completely and make a new mark.

After students have completed each test, review their answers. Note questions with which students have had difficulty, and help them find the appropriate details in the passage.

Answer Key

Page 26: 1. b, **2.** c, **3.** c, **4.** a
Page 27: 5. c, **6.** a, **7.** d, **8.** d, **9.** b
Page 28: 10. b, **11.** d, **12.** b, **13.** a, **14.** d
Page 29: 15. b, **16.** d, **17.** a, **18.** c, **19.** c, **20.** b

EXTENSION ACTIVITIES

The following are suggest activities to reinforce and enrich students' ability to identify details and the main idea:

1. Have students find magazine or newspaper photographs that show crowds of people at an event, either as participants or spectators. Use the photos to inspire writing activities in which students describe details in the photos and then summarize each photo's main idea in a one-sentence caption.

2. Have students choose favorite songs, write down some of the lyrics, and determine what theme, or main idea, the lyrics express. As an alternative, have students choose a theme that is common in songwriting—love, loneliness, or working, for example—and write down lyrics of songs that illustrate that theme.

3. Have students write a paragraph describing the most valuable thing they own. The first sentence should state the main idea of the paragraph. Encourage students to avoid the statement "The most valuable thing I own is _____," try instead for some variety of expression. (For example: "my record collection means more to me than any other thing I own.") The paragraph should also contain at least three details that give specific information about what is owned.

PART 2 □ INFERENCE

Introduction (Pages 30-31)

Objectives
Students will:
- focus on drawing inferences based on information in a reading selection.
- make inferences by reading a selection and answering multiple-choice questions.

Summary of Lesson Material
The photograph, selection, and exercise on pages 30-31 are a warm-up activity for making inferences.

The photograph on page 30 features a group of people, many with binoculars, gathered in a field to observe something. The selection on page 31 tells of using carrier pigeons as transporters of special delivery items; this is followed by three self-checking exercises.

Teaching Suggestions
Discuss with students the details in the photograph that indicate why the people have come together (for birdwatching). Then have students read the selection. As the students work with the questions, call attention to the words *apparently* and *probably*. Point out that these words indicate that the correct answers are not stated in the passage and that students must make inferences based on details that are given. Make sure students understand the meaning of *inference*. You may also wish to use the word *infer*, as in "What can you infer from the details in the passage?"

Answer Key
1. c, **2.** a, **3.** d

LESSON 1 □ Rapid Transit (Pages 32-33)

Objectives
Students will:
- analyze questions that require inferences.
- use details and main idea to answer inference questions.

Summary of Lesson Material
Wheelless trains, operating by magnetic force, can move at speeds of 300 mph. They are experimental.

Teaching Suggestions
The answer to each question is given and explained. Explain that in each lesson, students read a passage and figure out the correct answers to the questions, using details from the passage. By understanding the main idea and the details, students can determine what an author is saying. Emphasize that in order to make inferences, students must read for details and determine the main idea of a passage.

In **Lesson 1,** encourage students to complete each question before reading the **Check your answer** section that follows it. The **Check your answer** sections remind students of specific clues to inference questions, such as the word *probably,* as well as of strategies for using details in the selection to make inferences.

Answer Key
1. c, **2.** d, **3.** a, **4.** b

LESSON 2 □ Who Will Save the Rhino? (Pages 34-35)

Objectives
Students will:
■ analyze questions that require inferences.
■ use details and main idea to answer inference questions.

Summary of Lesson Material
African Rhinoceros meat and horns are used by Asians for many things. This could cause the extinction of the rhinoceros.

Teaching Suggestions
In **Lesson 2,** the answer appears after all the questions, so students may answer the questions on their own before checking their work. As you review the items, point out the word *probably* in items 1-3, signaling that an inference is to be made. A careful reading by students of the **Check your answer** section will reinforce the need to pay attention to details in making inferences.

Answer Key
1. c, **2.** c, **3.** a, **4.** b

LESSON 3 □ The Go-Team (Pages 36-37)

Objectives
Students will:
■ learn to make inferences by reading a selection and answering multiple choice questions.
■ recognize *most likely* as a signal that an inference is to be made.

Summary of Lesson Material
The Go-Team is a special unit of the National Transportation Safety Board used for investigating accidents. Members include experts on different aspects of the accident. The airline crash of 1982 in New Orleans is used as an example.

Teaching Suggestions
The **Check your answer** feature does not appear in **Lessons 3-12.** For each lesson, review the answers together after students have completed the exercise.

   In **Lesson 3,** call attention to the phrase *most likely* in item 2, another indication of an inference question. In addition to inference questions, this lesson also includes a question about details in the passage (item 1) and a main-idea question (item 4), allowing students an opportunity to review skills previously taught.

Answer Key
1. d, **2.** b, **3.** a, **4.** b, **5.** c, **6.** b

LESSON 4 □ The Company Town (Page 38-39)

Objectives
Students will:
■ make inferences by reading a selection and answering multiple choice questions.

Summary of Lesson Material
Gilchrist, Oregon is a town owned by Gilchrist Timber Company. It was established in the 1930's for the employees of this company.

Teaching Suggestions
In **Lesson 4,** students are required to infer a meaning from the context in item 3. Have them explain how they used details in the passage to make the correct inference. For item 6, have a volunteer explain the mathematics involved in determining the correct answer.

Answer Key
1. d, **2.** a, **3.** c, **4.** b, **5.** a, **6.** c

LESSON 5 □ Operator 802 (Pages 40-41)

Objectives
Students will:
■ make inferences by reading a selection and answering multiple-choice questions.
■ make inferences regarding a personal quality.

Summary of Lesson Material
Phyllis Hunter is a 911 operator in New York City. Like all 911 operators, she must accurately and quickly get information from the caller and transmit it via computer to a dispatcher.

Teaching Suggestions
In **Lesson 5,** call attention to the negative phrasing of item 5. Invite students to justify their answers to this question by using their own experience as well as details from the passage. Item 6 requires an inference about a personal quality, the subject of frequent questions on reading comprehension tests.

Answer Key
1. b, **2.** c, **3.** d, **4.** b, **5.** c, **6.** a

LESSON 6 □ The Day the Water Stopped (Pages 42-43)

Objectives
Students will:
■ draw inferences based on the understanding of the main idea and details of a selection.

Summary of Lesson Material
In July of 1982, the residents of Jersey City, New Jersey found themselves without water for a few days because an old pipe burst. The main valve at the

reservoir had to be turned off before repairs could be made. People there were helpful and resourceful in getting water for household use.

Teaching Suggestions
In **Lesson 6,** have volunteers explain how they used details to make inferences. For example, for item 2, ask a volunteer to read the details that indicate that shutting off the water supply at the reservoir was "the only possible solution" (choice **c**). Call attention to the phrase "The selection does not say" in item 4 and point out that all the other answer choices must be wrong in order for this one to be correct.

Answer Key
1. b, **2.** c, **3.** a, **4.** d, **5.** c

LESSON 7 □ Love, Care, and Herring (Pages 44-45)

Objectives
Students will:
- draw inferences based on the details and main idea of a selection.

Summary of Lesson Material
The California Marine Mammals Center rescues and treats all kinds of marine mammals. Petaluma is a northern fur seal who was aided by this group.

Teaching Suggestions
In **Lesson 7,** have students explain why the correct answer choice for item 1 is **c,** and not **a, b,** or **d.** Ask a volunteer to find the details in the third and fourth paragraphs that lead to the correct answer.

Answer Key
1. c, **2.** a, **3.** b, **4.** c, **5.** b, **6.** d

LESSON 8 □ Traveling Conversations (Pages 46-47)

Objectives
Students will:
- draw inferences based upon details and main idea of a selection.

Summary of Lesson Material
Cellular radio is the basis of car telephones and could replace regular phone service in remote, rural areas. Large metropolitan areas are divided into cells each having its own transmitter, allowing many clear connections. This type of communication is expensive.

Teaching Suggestions
In **Lesson 8,** five of the six items require students to complete a sentence. Suggest that students read the sentence starter with each answer choice before making a decision.

Answer Key
1. d, **2.** a, **3.** a, **4.** c, **5.** b, **6.** c

LESSON 9 □ The Dangling Boom (Pages 48-49)

Objectives
Students will:
- draw inferences based upon details and main idea of a selection.

Summary of Lesson Material
Three riggers, construction workers who handle cranes, risked their lives to prevent a crane that had separated from its tower from falling 44-stories to the street.

Teaching Suggestions
In **Lesson 9,** emphasize the fact that an answer choice may be incorrect yet seem reasonable. That is why students should verify an answer choice by checking details in the passage. In item 5, for example, choice **a** seems reasonable; however, students will know that this answer is false by checking the details in the last paragraph.

Answer Key
1. a, **2.** c, **3.** b, **4.** d, **5.** b

LESSON 10 □ The Electronic Doctor (Pages 50-51)

Objectives
Students will:
- draw inferences based upon details and main idea of a selection.

Summary of Lesson Material
Medical computer data bases can help doctors diagnose, treat, and develop more information about illnesses. There is such a computer at Duke University Medical Center in North Carolina.

Teaching Suggestions
In **Lesson 10,** caution students that choices **a** and **b** in item 5 are worded similarly, but should not be confused. Also, the format for item 6 is unusual because the question requires a *yes* or *no* answer. Point out to students that there are still four different answer choices.

Answer Key
1. c, **2.** a, **3.** c, **4.** d, **5.** b, **6.** d

LESSON 11 □ Cracking an Ancient "Code" (Pages 52-53)

Objectives
Students will:
- draw inferences based upon details and main idea of a selection.

Summary of Lesson Material
The writing of the Indus Valley civilization of 4,000 years ago is very difficult to decipher. Now, after much work and perseverance, scientists are slowly

beginning to translate the symbols by matching and testing the sounds and words with today's Indian languages. Some of the matches have been successful.

Teaching Suggestions
In **Lesson 11,** the passage and questions should be read carefully because the answer choices in some questions have many words in common.

Answer Key
1. c, **2.** d, **3.** b, **4.** d, **5.** c, **6.** a

LESSON 12 □ It's a Snap (Pages 54-56)

Objectives
Students will:
■ have practice in drawing inferences based on information in a longer selection that is written in the first person.

Summary of Lesson Material
In the battle of building the largest skyscraper in 1929-1930, Margaret Bourke-White, a photographer for *Fortune* magazine, took pictures 800 feet above the street on top of the Chrysler Building to disprove rumors about this building.

Teaching Suggestions
In **Lesson 12,** the selection is longer than the previous ones and is told in the first person. Students will need to read the introduction in order to understand the context. Encourage them to look back at the passage to find the appropriate details for answering the questions.

Answer Key
1. a, **2.** c, **3.** d, **4.** b, **5.** d, **6.** b, **7.** a, **8.** b

TAKING TESTS (Pages 57-59)

Objectives
Students will:
■ review the skills covered in the Reading Comprehension Unit with emphasis on inference skills.
■ show their familiarity with the standardized test format of the three reading comprehension review tests.

Summary of Taking Tests (Page 57)
Emotional crying can reduce suffering by ridding the body of harmful chemicals, according to Dr. William Frey, a scientist in St. Paul, Minnesota.

Summary of Taking Tests (Page 58)
The phonograph was a simultaneous invention, being developed by Thomas Edison using a cylinder and Emile Berliner using a flat disc. Berliner's idea took the lead and is used today.

Summary of Taking Tests (Page 59)
On a Night of Snow expresses the disadvantages the Mistress sees in her cat's desire to go outside in a snowstorm and the advantages the cat sees in being outdoors.

Teaching Suggestions
Before students begin the test pages, review briefly the skills they have learned: finding details, identifying a main idea, and making inferences. Read the directions and the **Test Tips** on the three test pages with students. If students are using answer sheets to record their answers (see pages 83-96 of this Manual), tell them to fill in the space that goes with the letter of the answer they choose. Point out that these tests are short; therefore, students will not have to fill in all the answer spaces.

Note that the second test (page 58) is a cloze test. Remind students to read each paragraph carefully before deciding which words to fill in. The third test (page 59) requires students to use details in a poem to make inferences. Encourage students to read the poem as they might read a story, looking for details and the main idea.

After students have completed the tests, review the answers and discuss any problems.

Answer Key
Page 57: 1. c, **2.** d, **3.** c, **4.** b
Page 58: 5. b, **6.** c, **7.** a, **8.** d, **9.** c, **10.** b
Page 59: 11. d, **12.** c, **13.** a, **14.** b, **15.** c

EXTENSION ACTIVITIES

The following are suggested activities to reinforce and enrich students' ability to make inferences.

1. Have students bring in an assortment of illustrated magazine ads for various products or services. They should tape over the name of the product and its description. Other students may the use clues in the drawing or photograph to infer the kind of product or service being advertised.

2. Have each student write a three-sentence description of a favorite movie or television series. The sentences should include details about the setting, characters, and situations. Neither the setting nor the characters should be named. Have class members infer the name of each movie or TV program.

3. On the board, write four items that present a pattern. Challenge students to infer the fifth item in the pattern by using the details given. For example:
(a) giant, large, medium, small _____ *(tiny)*
(b) $6, $12, $24, $48, _____ *($96)*
(c) aardvark, hobby, occur, caddy, _____ *(any word containing a double e)*
Have students make up their own patterns.

PART 3 ☐ CRITICAL READING

Introduction (Pages 60-61)

Objectives
Students will:
- focus on critical reading.
- practice the critical reading skills of determining a writer's purpose, evaluating opinions, recognizing points of view, and analyzing the validity and reliability of supporting details.

Summary of Lesson Material
The picture on page 60 of a man holding a skull is from a famous play. It is used here to evoke students' ideas about the author's opinions.

Page 61 presents a short selection on why people get ice cream headaches. It is followed by three self-checking questions.

Teaching Suggestions
The photograph, selection, and exercise on pages 60-61 are a warm-up activity for critical reading. Ask students to imagine what the character in the play might be saying. (Direct interested students to *Hamlet*, Act V, Scene 1, for Hamlet's opinions about Yorick, whose skull he holds.)

Point out that opinions are most persuasive when they are backed up by supporting details. In critical reading, students must judge a writer's opinion based on the details that are given.

After students have read the selection and completed the exercise, review the answers together.

Answer Key
1. b, **2.** a, **3.** c

LESSON 1 ☐ On Your Own (Pages 62-63)

Objectives
Students will:
- identify the nature of a passage.
- identify the purpose of an article.
- identify an author's opinion and find details to support that opinion.

Summary of Lesson Material
This selection details monthly expenses for which one should budget when planning to live independently.

Teaching Suggestions
Lessons 1 and 2 are self-checking practice lessons that lead students to an understanding of a selection through critical-reading skills. Explain that students will read a selection and determine the correct answers to the questions, using details from the story. In this lesson, the answer is given and explained after each question. Encourage students to answer each question before reading the accompanying **Check your answer** section.

Answer Key
1. b, **2.** d, **3.** a, **4.** c

LESSON 2 □ How 55 Saves Lives (Pages 64-65)

Objectives
Students will:
- use critical reading skills to answer questions about a selection.
- test the reliability of details in answering critical reading questions.

Summary of Lesson Material
In 1974, the U.S. Congress passed a law that required states to set 55 miles per hour as the maximum speed limit on their highways. The law has saved fuel and lives.

Teaching Suggestions
In this lesson, the answers are grouped together after all the questions, so students may answer the questions on their own before checking their work.

Remind students that critical reading often involves testing the reliability of details that support opinions. Discuss with students the ways in which figures are used to support the opinions of the writer. Emphasize the importance of knowing the source of the figures used in the passage. Remind students of the differences between facts and opinions, and have students consider how facts from the article could be checked.

Answer Key
1. c, **2.** a, **3.** c, **4.** b

LESSON 3 □ The Panda Watch (Pages 66-67)

Objectives
Students will:
- practice critical-reading skills by using details in the passage to check their validity.

Summary of Lesson Material
This selection tells how scientist George Schaller researched the habits of Pandas to save them from extinction and to help keep them alive in captivity. An ancient legend about Pandas is also given.

Teaching Suggestions
The **Check your Answer** feature does not appear in this lesson or the following lessons in Part 3. For each lesson, review the answers together after students have completed the exercise.

The students practice critical-reading skills by using details in the passage to check the validity of a scientist's conclusions. Ask students if all scientists are likely to have the same opinions about pandas, and if not, why not. In reviewing item 3, ask students to explain why scientists would have difficulty proving that a panda's solitary life leads to loneliness.

Answer Key
1. c, **2.** d, **3.** c, **4.** d, **5.** b

LESSON 4 ☐ Good Tunes (Pages 68-69)

Objectives
Students will:
- use details and draw inferences to answer critical reading questions.

Summary of Lesson Material
Alberta Hunter, a great blues singer, performed until her death at the age of 89.

Teaching Suggestions
The selection is a biography of a performer that includes opinions about her music. Have students locate details in the passage that the writer uses to support the opinions. Call attention to the words *probably* and *apparently* in items 3, 4, and 5, signaling an inference. Remind students that part of critical reading involves making inferences about an author's opinions.

Answer Key
1. b, 2. c, 3. a, 4. b, 5. d, 6. b

LESSON 5 ☐ Is There a Place for You in Broadcasting? (Pages 70-71)

Objectives
Students will:
- focus on the author's purpose as an important critical-reading skill.

Summary of Lesson Material
This selection tells how one can get started in broadcasting. It also lists the many aspects of broadcasting in which one can work.

Teaching Suggestions
This lesson provides an opportunity for students to focus on the author's purpose as a critical-reading skill. Explain that one way of phrasing a question about the author's purpose is "This article was written mainly to _____," as in item 1. ("Why was the article written?" is another possible variant.) Determining an author's purpose requires an understanding of which opinions are expressed and how the opinions are supported.

Answer Key
1. d, 2. b, 3. c, 4. a, 5. c

LESSON 6 ☐ The Great Hunting Debate (Pages 72-73)

Objectives
Students will:
- use critical-reading skills to analyze two letters with opposing points of view.

Summary of Lesson Material
Two letters present opinions about hunting. One letter to a newspaper is by a hunter supporting his sport as a tool for wildlife protection and conservation, keeping nature in balance. The other letter claims hunting to be cruel and not a sport because two sides are not equally competing.

Teaching Suggestions

Lesson 6 presents two letters that take opposing points of view about hunting. Introduce the selection by calling attention to the title and explain that the word *debate* suggests that two sides of an issue will be presented. Point out that items 2, 4, and 5 require and understanding of the details in *both* letters. For item 5, students will have to know which answer choices *are* covered by hunting regulations to know which one is not.

Answer Key
1. a, **2.** c, **3.** b, **4.** b, **5.** d

LESSON 7 □ A Fire Fighter Speaks Out (Pages 74-75)

Objectives
Students will:
■ use critical-reading skills to answer multiple-choice questions.

Summary of Lesson Material
A fire fighter tells of the tragedy of a child's death in a fire. He urges the use of smoke detectors and fire education.

Teaching Suggestions
In **Lesson 7,** students should guess immediately from the title that the author of the article is a fire fighter; details from the passage will reinforce that notion and will lead to a correct answer for item 1. Also, explain that incorrect answer choices often contain details from the passage, but that those details may not be the ones needed to answer the question. In item 2, for example, the term *smoke detector* in choice **b** might lead students to make that choice. However, a careful reading of all the answer choices should help them realize that **c** is the only one that is entirely correct. Have students point to details in the passage that supported the answer to item 6.

Answer Key
1. b, **2.** c, **3.** a, **4.** d, **5.** c, **6.** b

TAKING TESTS (Pages 76-78)

Objectives
Students will:
■ review the skills taught in the previous seven lessons: reading critically to determine a writer's purpose, opinions, and details that support those opinions.

Summary of Test Material (Page 76)
This selection discusses the effects of caffeine on the body and suggests reducing its intake.

Summary of Test Material (Page 77)
Automatically "breathing" teddy bears placed in cribs of babies known to have faulty breathing are being used experimentally to help create regular breathing rhythms in these babies.

Summary of Test Material (Page 78)
In this poem the author relates his reflections on life when he crushes a mite with his nail while writing.

Teaching Suggestions
Read the directions on page 76 with the students. Call attention to the **Test Tips** that precede the tests. If students are using answer sheets to record their answers (see pages 83-96 of this Manual), tell them to fill in the space that goes with the letter of the answer they choose.

Note that the third test (page 78) requires students to analyze a writer's opinions and feelings in a poem. Encourage students to look for details in the poem that will help indicate the poet's opinions.

After students have completed the tests, review their answers and discuss items with which they had particular problems.

Answer Key
Page 76: 1. b, **2.** d, **3.** c, **4.** b
Page 77: 5. b, **6.** d, **7.** a, **8.** b, **9.** d
Page 78: 10. b, **11.** a, **12.** c, **13.** d

EXTENSION ACTIVITIES

The following are suggested activities to reinforce and enrich students' ability to use critical-reading skills:

1. Follow up **Lesson 6** by organizing a class debate on whether or not hunting should be permitted. Members of opposing teams should develop ideas of their own to supplement the arguments in the lesson. Supporting details can be provided through research on the topic. Each side should be allowed an alloted time for making its argument. Class members could then decide which team presented the most effective argument.

2. What kind of a world do students expect to see by the year 2000? Have them write their predictions, focusing on one particular aspect of society, such as schools, jobs, or leisure-time activities. Students should draw on evidence of present-day changes in society to make their visions of the future as realistic as possible.

3. Start an "Opinion Line" bulletin board. use the title "Opinion of the Day" at the top of the board. Every day for a week post an opinion about which students are likely to differ. (For example: "Students should get extra credit for taking hard courses" or "The school day should be extended." [The subject can also reflect broader concerns.]) Ask students to decide whether they agree or disagree with the opinion and to write several statements that either support or refute it. Have seveal of these read aloud and invite comments. Post students' writings under sections of the bulletin board headed "pro" and "con." After the first week, have a volunteer compose the "opinion of the day" and post it.

4. If a camera is available, invite students to be "inquiring photographers." Have rotating photographer/reporter teams interview teachers and othger students about their reactions to specific questions. (The questions should be chosen by the entire class.) The responses collected could be written up and submitted, along with the photos, to the school newspaper or a community newspaper.

UNIT II Vocabulary

PART 1 □ SYNONYMS AND ANTONYMS

Introduction (Page 80)

Objectives
Students will:
- focus on two different strategies for comprehending the meanings of new words.

Summary of Lesson Material
The drawing on page 80 is an introduction to the two techniques used in this part of the unit.

Teaching Suggestions
Discuss which book titles express similar information (*Developing a Thriving Commercial Establishment; Creating a Successful Business*) and which expresses opposite information (*A Collection of Important Information; A Digest of Insignificant Details*). Go over pairs of synonyms (*developing—creating, thriving—sucessful, commercial—business, collection—digest*) and antonyms (*important—insignificant*). Point out that the other two titles are neither similar nor opposite. Explain that words can be thought of as names or titles for ideas. Sometimes two words name the same idea. At other times, two words may name opposite ideas.

SYNONYMS AND MEANING (Pages 81-83)

Objectives
Students will:
- complete exercise using synonyms.
- use a synonym of a new word as the simplest way to explain the meaning.

Summary of Lesson Material
Two selections are presented followed by exercises. The passage on page 81 tells that, when his door-to-door bookselling business failed in 1886, D.H. McConnell had a line of toilet articles made. He devised a network of sales representatives to distribute his new products. He named his company Avon. The passage on page 84 is about King Gillette who invented the disposable razor blade.

Teaching Suggestions
Synonyms are invaluable tools for helping students understand the meanings of words. The definition of a word is often expressed as a one- or two-word synonym. Identifying synonyms is a basic way for students to demonstrate how well they comprehend a word's meaning.

Read page 81 with the students. Discuss why it helps to replace the harder words (*vend, prosper, concoction*) with the easier ones (*sell, succeed, mixture*). Then have the students complete the exercises on pages 82-83. In exercise A and B, emphasize that the sentences must make sense after the original words have been replaced by the students' answer choices. Also encourage students to think of other synonyms that could be substituted for each new word in the selections.

Exercise C is a self-checking review of six of the new words presented in the earlier exercises. Students are introduced to the format used in many vocabulary achievement tests. Point out that substitution of words will not always help in this exercise since full sentences are not given.

Answer Key
A. 1. d, **2.** b, **3.** e, **4.** a, **5.** c
B. 1. laborious, **2.** affluent, **3.** implement, **4.** conceived, **5.** disposable
C. 1. c, **2.** a, **3.** b, **4.** b, **5.** a, **6.** c

LESSON 1 □ The First President (Pages 84-85)

Objectives
Students will:
■ use synonyms to complete sentences.
■ will identify the synonyms of new words used in phrases or sentences.

Summary of Lesson Material
From 1781 to 1789, a president was chosen each year to preside over the meetings of congress under the Articles of Confederation.

Teaching Suggestions
Begin **Lesson 1** by discussing the eight new words with the students. Point out that many of the new words are related to government and lawmaking. Point out that some words can be remembered more easily when they are associated with a common idea or theme. Also discuss the concept of trying to relate new words with other words that seem to have similar parts. For example, *unified* and *united* begin the same way; *preside* is contained within the word *president*; and *statesman* includes the word *state*. Students will learn more about recognizing and using word parts in Part 4 of this unit.

Review the answers to exercises A and B for each lesson in Part 1. Students who are having difficulty with one or more of the new words should be encouraged to review the reading selection to see how the problem words were used in context. For exercise C, have students suggest ways to start each sentence so that the vocabulary word is used. (For example: 1. Gerald Ford's *successors* as U.S. president have been _____.) Have volunteers read their sentences aloud. Encourage students to write additional sentences using the five other lesson words.

If you wish, suggest that students use the Glossary on pages 218-220 of the student book to check their answers for these and all future activities in this unit.

Answer Key
1. decayed, improved; **2.** improved, worsened; **3.** hopeful, discouraged;
4. unalike, similar; **5.** yielded, kept; **6.** eagerness, patience;
7. prohibited, permitted; **8.** true, false; **9.** departed, arrived; **10.** rough, smooth
B. 1. b, **2.** c, **3.** a, **4.** c
C. Answers will vary.

LESSON 2 □ A Castle of Mysteries (Pages 86-87)

Objectives
Students will:
■ use synonyms to complete sentences.
■ identify the synonyms of new words used in phrases or sentences.

- identify words with the same ending as being a particular part of speech giving a clue to meaning.

Summary of Lesson Material
Actor William Gillette, who portrayed Sherlock Holmes more then 1,300 times on stage, built a castle in Connecticut that is very mysterious. It is filled with mazes, mirrors, secret panels, and other features copied from the Holmes' stories.

Teaching Suggestions
When introducing the new vocabulary in **Lesson 2,** point out the relationship between the words *fictional* and *portrayed* and the words *fiction* and *portrait*. Once again, point out the value of looking for word parts as meaning clues. Ask students to identify the two words in the lesson with the same ending— *portrayed* and *converted*. Explain that the *ed* ending often indicates that the word is an action word, or verb, in the past tense.

Answer Key
A. 1. elude, **2.** portrayed, **3.** converted, **4.** fascination, **5.** traits, **6.** fictional, **7.** impressive, **8.** elaborate
B. 1. c, **2.** b, **3.** b, **4.** c
C. Answers will vary.

LESSON 3 □ Diet Drinks Are Big Business (Pages 88-89)

Objectives
Students will:
- use synonyms to identify the meaning of new words.
- group words around theme of selling.

Summary of Lesson Material
This selection tells how diet sodas, specifically TAB, came into being.

Teaching Suggestions
Several of the new words in **Lesson 3** can be associated with selling. Ask students to identify any of the new words that deal with this theme. Also encourage students to relate several of the new words with words they already know that look like the new words (for example, *anxiety* and anxious, merchandising and *merchant, escalate* and *escalator)*. Ask students to explain how the meanings of each pair of words are related.

Answer Key
A. 1. exclusively, **2.** emphasis, **3.** beverages, **4.** merchandising, **5.** percentage, **6.** escalate, **7.** anxiety, **8.** dwindling
B. 1. c, **2.** b, **3.** b, **4.** a
C. Answers will vary.

LESSON 4 □ Japanese Prison Camps in the United States (Pages 90-91)

Objectives
Students will:
- focus on a central theme—law and order.
- use synonyms to identify the meaning of new words.

Summary of Lesson Material

After the attack on Pearl Harbor by the Japanese in 1941, Japanese Americans were gathered and incarcerated for the duration of the war.

Teaching Suggestions

Discuss how associating words such as *security, incarcerated, decree,* and *unjust* with this theme can help students remember their meanings. You might also point out the *ed* ending on both *incarcerated* and *disbanded,* indicate verbs in the past tense. In addition, you might want to discuss how the negative prefixes in *disbanded* and *unjust* turn these words into antonyms of *banded* and *just.* Students will learn more about looking for negative prefixes in the antonym section of Part 1 (pages 96-104).

Answer Key

A. **1.** incarcerated, **2.** compensate, **3.** invade, **4.** unjust, **5.** abet, **6.** security, **7.** disbanded, **8.** decree
B. **1.** b, **2.** c, **3.** a, **4.** c
C. Answers will vary.

LESSON 5 □ TV for the Deaf (Pages 92-94)

Objectives

Students will:
■ use synonyms to determine the meaning of words.

Summary of Lesson Material

Closed captions, or sound translated into printed captions that appear on a TV screen, help the deaf to enjoy TV. A decoder to attach to the television to add the written captions on the screen can be purchased.

Teaching Suggestions

In **Lesson 5,** discuss which new words relate to hearing *(dialogue, audio)* or to mental processes *(noticeable, interpret, surmise).* You might also point out that *curtail* and *expedite* are nearly opposite in meaning.

Students who want to know more about closed captioning for the hearing impaired can write directly to the National Captioning Institute at Suite 1500, 5303 Leesburg Pike, Falls Church, VA 20041.

Answer Key

A. **1.** audio, **2.** dialogue, **3.** curtail, **4.** noticeable, **5.** impaired, **6.** options, **7.** expenditure, **8.** surmise, **9.** expedite, **10.** interpret
B. **1.** c, **2.** a, **3.** c, **4.** b
C. Answers will vary.

WORD REVIEW (Page 95)

Objectives

Students will:
■ review ten of the new vocabulary words form the previous five lessons.

Summary of Lesson Material

Two words have been selected from each lesson. Students use each new word to replace a synonym in one of the review sentences.

Teaching Suggestions
Encourage students actually to rewrite the sentence to reinforce their ability to
use the new words.

  After students have completed the exercise, review the answers together.
Encourage students to read each sentence, using the vocabulary word. As an
additional activity, students may make up their own sentences using
synonyms for other lesson words, and then challenge classmates to replace
the synonyms with the new vocabulary words they have learned.

Answer Key
1. unified, **2.** authority, **3.** impressive, **4.** elaborate, **5.** percentage, **6.** merchandising, **7.** incarcerated, **8.** abet, **9.** dialogue, **10.** noticeable

ANTONYMS AND MEANING (Pages 96-97)

Objectives
Students will:
- be shown how antonyms are valuable tools for understanding vocabulary.
- define unfamiliar words by thinking of a contrasting or contradictory idea.

Summary of Lesson Material
Page 96 introduces antonyms and meaning by presenting prefixes that when
added to a word change it to its opposite. This is followed by a selection and
exercise about Proctor and Gamble's Ivory soap. Page 97 presents a passage
about Dixie Cups followed by two self-checking exercises.

Teaching Suggestions
Read through page 96 with the students. Point out that the prefix *un, in, im
dis,* or *non* before a word often, but not always means "not." Examples when
the prefix does not mean "not" include: *unanimous, invest, impact, discuss,* and
nonagon. The rest of the world after the prefix may help students determine if
the prefix means "not."

  Have students complete the exercises on pages 96 and 97. Discuss the idea
of how a word can be defined as the opposite of another word. For example,
indigent can mean "not wealthy" or "poor." In the same way, *vigorously* can
mean "not weakly," or "strongly" and so on. Let volunteers point out the
vocabulary words and antonyms that start with a negative prefix. Caution
students to read the directions to exercise B carefully before completing the
items.

Answer Key
Page 96: 1. strongly, **2.** unhappy or annoyed, **3.** not floating or sinking
Page 97: A. 1. inexpensive, **2.** impure, **3.** foremost, **4.** enormous, **5.** unsanitary
B. 1. c, **2.** a, **3.** b, **4.** c

LESSON 6 ☐ Cities on the Rise (Pages 98-99)

Objectives
Students will:
- match vocabulary words with their antonyms.
- identify antonyms of new words used in phrases or sentences.

Summary of Lesson Material
Older cities in the U.S. have experienced a decline in population and monies needed to revitalize their inner business districts. With the help of federal money this is changing.

Teaching Suggestions
In **Lesson 6,** read and discuss the new words with students. Emphasize that the word(s) beside each new word is a synonym, not an antonym. Call attention to the fact that most of the lesson words deal with run-down conditions or with a sense of improvement. Ask students which words have negative connotations *(insufficient, declining, deteriorated)* and which have positive connotations *(upgraded, optimistic).* Also have students identify four words that start with negative prefixes. Discuss how the prefixes convert the base words into their antonyms. You might also also students to identify the two new words that are antonyms of each other *(upgraded, deteriorated).*

For all three antonym lessons, go over the students' antonym matches for exercise A and multiple-choice answers for exercise B. Remind students who have difficulty with a word to see how it was used in the story. Also discuss different ways to begin sentences for exercise C so that they include the lesson words.

Answer Key
A. 1. deteriorated, **2.** declining, **3.** nonexistent, **4.** optimistic, **5.** discontinued, **6.** insufficient, **7.** unoccupied, **8.** upgraded
B. 1. a, **2.** b, **3.** b, **4.** c
C. Answers will vary.

LESSON 7 □ New Life in a New Land (Pages 100-101)

Objectives
Students will:
- match vocabulary words with their antonyms.
- review prefixes meaning "not".

Summary of Lesson Material
Cuban born Manolo Reyes made a good life in the U.S. after fleeing Castro's Cuba in the 1960's. He is helping other Hispanics in this country.

Teaching Suggestions
When introducing the new vocabulary in **Lesson 7,** have students note those words starting with a prefix meaning "not" *(dissimilar, impatience, inhospitable).* Point out that the suffix *less,* meaning "without," also gives a word a negative meaning. Thus, *penniless* means "without a penny" or "broke." Have students identify the synonyms for the lesson words that also contain a negative prefix or suffix *(unlike* for *dissimilar, unkind* for *inhospitable, restlessness* for *impatience).* Discuss the idea that some of the base words *(alike—similar* and *kind—hospitable)* are probably synonyms.

Answer Key
A. 1. inhospitable, **2.** relinquished, **3.** passionate, **4.** impatience, **5.** forbade, **6.** wrangled, **7.** penniless, **8.** dissimilar
B. 1. b, **2.** c, **3.** a, **4.** a
C. Answers will vary.

LESSON 8 □ Reliving a Legend (Pages 102-104)

Objectives
Students will:
- match new words with antonyms in isolation.
- identify antonyms for the lesson words as they are used in sentences.

Summary of Lesson Material
Tim Severin writes adventure stories about the deeds of renowned explorers. Before he writes, Severin relives the adventures himself. This passage tells of his adventure to relive St. Brendan's journey Across the North Atlantic.

Teaching Suggestions
Read and discuss the new words with students. Ask them which words have a positive connotation (*renowned, valiant*) and which have a negative connotation (*turbulent, treacherous, unappealing, disheartened*). Also, call attention to the new words or their synonyms that begin with negative prefixes. You might also ask students to name which pair of words are nearly antonyms of each other (*factual, implausible*).

Answer Key
A. **1.** treacherous, **2.** embarked, **3.** impassable, **4.** turbulent, **5.** disheartened, **6.** factual, **7.** unappealing, **8.** implausible, **9.** renowned, **10.** valiant
B. **1.** b, **2.** a, **3.** b, **4.** c, **5.** c, **6.** a
C. Answers will vary.

WORD REVIEW (Page 105)

Objectives
Students will:
- review ten of the new words from the previous three lessons.

Summary of Lesson Material
Students provide both a synonym and an antonym for each new word that is used in a sentence.

Teaching Suggestions
After students have completed the exercise, review the answers together. Encourage students to read each sentence, using their synonym choice, to see if the sentence still makes sense. Then have them read the sentence with their antonym choice to see how the sentence makes negative sense or no sense at all. As an additional activity, students may make up their own sentences using other new words from **Lesson 6-8.**

Answer Key
1. decayed, improved; **2.** improved, worsened; **3.** hopeful, discouraged; **4.** unalike, similar; **5.** yielded, kept; **6.** eagerness, patience; **7.** prohibited, permitted; **8.** true, false; **9.** departed, arrived; **10.** rough, smooth

TAKING TESTS (Pages 106-109)

Objectives
Students will:
- become familiar with the different formats of standardized vocabulary tests.

■ show mastery of the vocabulary words and skills covered in the previous eight lessons.

Summary of Taking Tests (Page 106)
Students will identify the meaning of a new word used in a phrase; there are ten phrases.

Summary of Taking Tests (Page 107)
Students will complete a sentence, using a synonym of a new word; there are ten sentences.

Summary of Taking Tests (Page 108)
Students will identify the antonym of a new word used in a phrase; there are ten phrases.

Summary of Taking Tests (Page 109)
Students will complete a sentence, using an antonym of a new word; there are ten sentences.

Teaching Suggestions
Read the **Test Tips** with the students. Remind them to read the directions for each test carefully, since some tests require identifying synonyms and others require identifying antonyms. If students are using answer sheets to record their answers (see pages 83-96 of this Manual), tell them to fill in the space on the answer sheet that corresponds with the item number and answer choice letter. To change an answer, students must erase the old mark completely and make a new mark.

Have students check their answers as they finish each test or after completing all four. Note any difficulties, and review. You might also want to discuss the different question formats so that students will recognize them on achievement tests they may take later.

Answer Key
Page 106: 1. c, **2.** b, **3.** a, **4.** c, **5.** c, **6.** c, **7.** a, **8.** d, **9.** b, **10.** b
Page 107: 11. c, **12.** a, **13.** b, **14.** d, **15.** b, **16.** d, **17.** c, **18.** a, **19.** c, **20.** d
Page 108: 21. d, **22.** b, **23.** a, **24.** d, **25.** b, **26.** a, **27.** c, **28.** d, **29.** d, **30.** b
Page 109: 31. d, **32.** b, **33.** b, **34.** c, **35.** d, **36.** a **37.** b, **38.** d, **39.** c, **40.** c

EXTENSION ACTIVITIES

These are suggested activities to reinforce and enrich vocabulary skills using synonyms and antonyms:

1. Have students write newspaper headlines, using synonyms to replace key words. (For example: "Legislators Meet To Discuss Budget Proposal" could be rewritten as "Lawmakers Gather To Talk About Budget Suggestions.") Have volunteers read their "synonym headlines" aloud to see if classmates can guess the phrasing of the originals.

2. Play "Synonym Bingo." Have students write 25 of the new words from Lessons 1-8 into boxes of a 5 x 5 grid. Then call out synonyms for many of the new words. Students check off new words on their grids that match the synonyms. The first student to get five in a row horizontally, vertically, or diagonally wins. (Alternative: Play "Antonym Bingo.")

PART 2 □ CONTEXT CLUES

Introduction (Pages 110-113)

Objectives
Students will:
- focus on the use of context clues to determine the meaning of a new word in a selection.
- work with five types of context clues to help them infer the meaning of new words.

Summary of Lesson Material
On page 110 a picture of an old church is the context from which the definition of DILAPIDATED is elicited. Pages 111-113 present the five context clues that will be used in this part of the vocabulary unit. A selection for each clue is followed by a **Check your answer** feature.

Teaching Suggestions
Remind students that in Part 1 they were given the meanings of the lesson words before reading the selections. Explain that in Part 2 the new words will not be defined first. Rather, students will look for clues in the reading selection to help them figure out the meaning of new words. Additional hints will be provided in exercise A of each lesson.

By recognizing a synonym or an antonym in context, students can apply the skills they learned in Part 1 to help them determine the meanings of new words in Part 2.

The introductory material on pages 110-113 is self-checking. After students have studied the picture, have them explain what helped them decide the meaning of *dilapidated*. Point out that a story, like a picture, can hold clues that will help students understand the meanings of unfamiliar words. As students read the first selection on page 111, emphasize that the meaning of *banned* is hidden somewhere in the passage. Go over the explanation beneath the passage to make sure students understand how to apply context clues.

The five additional passages on pages 111-113 explain five types of context clues that students can use to help determine a word's meaning. Read the explanation of each clue with the students. For clues 1 and 3, have students look for the meaning of each new word in the passage. For clues 2, 4, and 5, emphasize that the word's meaning does not actually appear in the passage. Students have to infer the meaning based on the context in which the word is used. Answers are provided in the **Check your answer** section after each passage.

LESSON 1 □ The Disaster Business (Pages 114-115)

Objectives
Students will:
- use context clues to determine the meaning of the new words in a selection.

Summary of Lesson Material
Ron Alford has created a business called Disaster Masters Inc. which specializes in doing restorations after a disaster.

Teaching Suggestions
Since this lesson introduces new types of exercises involving the use of context clues students may benefit from a teacher-directed lesson. Have students

define any new words they recognize. Then have them read through the entire selection to get a general sense of the article and how the new words are used. Review the types of context clues described on pages 111-113. Also discuss how many of the lesson words can be associated with the ideas of disasters and their correction.

Guide the students question by question through exercise A. Then review their answers to exercise B, pointing out that the synonyms can be found among the answer choices in exercise A. For additional practice in exercise C, have students write questions and answers using the other new words in Lesson 1.

Answer Key
A. 1. c, 2. c, 3. b, 4. a, 5. b, 6. b, 7. c, 8. c
B. 1. catastrophes—disasters, 2. exasperate—upset, 3. rectify—repair
4. conceived—thought up, 5. revenue—income, 6. reek—odor, 7. expunge—erase, 8. horrendous—terrible
C. Answers will vary.

LESSON 2 ☐ Farming for Oil (Pages 116-117)

Objectives
Students will:
▪ use context clues to determine the meaning of new words in a selection.

Summary of Lesson Material
Canadian scientists are growing and experimenting with special organisms called "petrobugs" that turn air and sunshine into oil.

Teaching Suggestions
In **Lesson 2,** read and discuss the new words with the students. have students locate them in the reading selection to see how they are used. Encourage students to use word parts to relate several of the new words to words they already know or have learned in previous lessons. For example, *organisms* contains *organ; unison* and *unified* (Part 1, Lesson 1) begin the same way; *extracted* and *subtracted* could be related; and *expended* and *expenditure* (Part 1, Lesson 5) seem closely connected. Also point out that *crisis* and the word *catastrophe* from the previous lesson are nearly synonyms.

Answer Key
A. 1. b, 2. c, 3. c, 4. a, 5. b, 6. a, 7. c, 8. b
B. 1. petroleum—oil, 2. unconventional—unusual, 3. organisms—living creatures, 4. deficiency—shortage, 5. unison—togetherness, 6. extracted—removed, 7. expended—consumed, 8. crisis—disaster
C. Answers will vary

LESSON 3 ☐ Joining the Circus (Pages 118-119)

Objectives
Students will:
▪ use context clues to determine the meaning of new words in a selection.

Summary of Lesson Material
This selection tells the procedure for joining the circus. Details about the circus lifestyle are included.

Teaching Suggestions
In discussing the new words in **Lesson 3,** point out that *auditions* and *audio*

(Part 1, Lesson 5) are closely related. Students might use a dictionary to discover the connection. Also discuss how *minority* and *minor*, and *applicants* and *apply* are related. You might also want to bring out the idea that *engaged* has two very different meanings. Students will learn more about multiple-meaning words in Part 3 of this unit.

Answer Key
A. 1. 1, 2. b, 3. b, 4. c, 5. a, 6. c, 7. b, 8. b
B. 1. enroll—sign up, 2. applicants—candidates, 3. auditions—trials,
4. minority—few 5. engaged—hired, 6. glamorous—fascinating, 7. vacate—leave,
8. grueling—difficult
C. Answers will vary.

LESSON 4 ☐ The Wise and Humble King (Pages 120-121)

Objectives
Students will:
■ use context clues to determine the meaning of new words in a selection.

Summary of Lesson Material
The King of Swaziland for 82 years was Sobhuza. He was an enlightened, humble ruler who kept his country happy and united by respecting their traditions and introducing technology where needed.

Teaching Suggestions
When introducing new words in **Lesson 4,** call attention to the negative prefix in *incapable.* Also ask volunteers to discuss how *sovereign* is related to *reign*, or *enlightened* to *light.* (For example, ask students what the expression "to see the light" means.) You might also discuss the powerful connotations of *abolished* and point out that it is a synonym of *expunge* (Part 2, Lesson 1).
   Review students' answers to exercises A and B in each of these four lessons. Have them identify the type of clue they used in each item. Then have volunteers read their sentences for exercise C.

Answer Key
A. 1. a, 2. c, 3. b, 4. c, 5. c, 6. b, 7. a, 8. c
B. 1. incapable—unable, 2. sovereign—ruler, 3. humble—modest, 4. shunned—avoided, 5. enlightened—wise, 6. pragmatic—practical, 7. abolished—canceled,
8. revered—respected
C. Answers will vary.

WORD REVIEW (Page 122)

Objectives
Students will:
■ review ten of the new words from the previous four lessons.

Summary of Lesson Material
Students complete ten sentences, each with a lesson word. They use a context clue in each sentence to help them make their selection.

Teaching Suggestions
Encourage students to actually rewrite the complete sentences to reinforce their ability to use the new words.
   Review answers aloud after students have completed the review. Have volunteers explain what context clues helped them make their decision for each sentence. As an additional activity, students may make up more sentences using other lesson words, and then challenge classmates to fill in the appropriate new word from a group of three choices.

Answer Key
1. exasperate, 2. rectify, 3. deficiency, 4. extracted, 5. unison, 6. auditions,
7. vacate, 8. minority, 9. sovereign, 10. revered

TAKING TESTS (Pages 123-125)

Objectives
Students will:
- become familiar with several different vocabulary test formats.
- show mastery of the vocabulary words and skills covered in the previous four lessons.

Summary of Taking Tests (Page 123)
In this test students identify synonyms for new words used in phrases. There are ten phrases given.

Summary of Taking Tests (Page 124)
Students identify synonyms for new words used in sentences. There are eight sentences given.

Summary of Taking Tests (Page 125)
This test does not involve words previously introduced in the unit. Instead, it required students to infer the meanings of six new words presented in a reading-selection context about the value of violins.

Teaching Suggestions
Review the **Test Tips** and read the directions with students before they begin. If students are using answer sheets to record their answers (see pages 83-96 of this Manual), tell them to fill in the space on the answer sheet that corresponds with the item number and answer choice letter. Point out that not all the spaces on the answer sheet will be filled in for these tests.

   After students have completed each test, or all three, review the answers together. Note which words or context clues gave students particular difficulty, and review.

Answer Key
Page 123: 1. c, **2.** b, **3.** b, **4.** d, **5.** c, **6.** d, **7.** a, **8.** b, **9.** d, **10.** b
Page 124: 11. b, **12.** c, **13.** d, **14.** b, **15.** d, **16.** a, **17.** d, **18.** b
Page 125: 19. c, **20.** d, **21.** a, **22.** c, **23.** b, **24.** b

EXTENSION ACTIVITIES

The following activities are suggested to reinforce and enrich students' skills in recognizing and using context clues:

1. Have students copy a short paragraph from a newspaper or magazine article or ad. They should replace one key word in the paragraph with a word that doesn't fit, and then see if a classmate can spot the wrong word and figure out the right one. (Alternative: Students can leave a key word blank and give three choices for filling in the blank.)

2. Have each student clip an article from a newspaper or magazine on a subject the student doesn't know much about. The article should contain at least three to five words with which the student is unfamiliar. The student should try to infer the meaning of each word new word from its context, and then use a dictionary to see if the inference was correct.

PART 3 ☐ WORDS WITH SEVERAL MEANINGS

Introduction (Pages 126-129)

Objectives
Students will:
- be presented multiple-meaning words.
- determine the correct meaning of a word based on its context in a reading selection.

Summary of Lesson Material
The picture on page 126 illustrates the meanings of the word landing. Pages 127-129 present four self-checking exercises to show students how to determine which meaning will be appropriate with the word's context.

Teaching Suggestions
Remind students that in Part 2, they used context clues to figure out the meaning of new words. Sometimes the clue was based on experience, or what seemed to make sense. Explain that in Part 3, students will continue to use experience clues to help them decide on the appropriate meanings of new words.

Read page 126 with the students and discuss the three meanings of the word *landing* that are illustrated—(a) settling to the ground from the air, (b) the flat surface between two sets of stairs, and (c) a dock or pier.

Through the self-checking exercises on page 127, students determine how much they already know about multiple-meaning words. Have students complete the first exercise and tell what context clues helped them choose their answers. Encourage students to substitute their answer choices in the sentences to see if they make sense. For the second exercise, you might set up a contest to see how many different meanings students can come up with for each word.

Pages 128-129 are also self-checking practice pages. Discuss the context clues that helped students determine their answers.

Answer Key
Page 127: 1. b, **2.** a, **3.** d, **4.** c
Pages 128-129: A. 1; **B.** 1. a, **2.** b, **3.** b, **4.** a
C. 1. a, **2.** b, **3.** a, **4.** a, **5.** b, **6.** a

LESSON 1 ☐ Free Flying Pages (130-131)

Objectives
Students will:
- use context clues to help determine the meaning of a word that fits the context.

Summary of Lesson Material
Billy Olsen is one of the world's greatest pole vaulters. The technique of pole vaulting and Billy's travel experience with his vaulting pole are discussed in this selection.

Teaching Suggestions
In each of these three discussions, read and discuss the new words with the students. Emphasize that although each new word has at least two meanings, only one meaning will apply in the reading selection.

Since **Lesson 1** introduces students to a new set of skills and a new exercise format, they may benefit from a teacher-directed lesson. Ask students which words deal with physical movement *(vault, flexible, ascent, arch, plummet)*. This association may help them remember the words. You might point out the difference in part of speech between *ascent* and *ascent,* and the fact that *ascend* is an antonym of *plummet.*

Encourage students to look back at the story to find context clues for each item in exercise A. Review the answers to exercise B. For additional practice in exercise C, students may write questions using the same words but with different meanings. (For example: 1. What was your *ultimate* action before leaving for school today?)

Answer Key
A. **1.** b, **2.** a, **3.** a, **4.** b, **5.** b, **6.** a, **7.** b, **8.** b
B. **1.** vault, **2.** arch, **3.** conviction, **4.** flexible
C. Answers will vary.

LESSON 2 ☐ Coupon Clippers (Pages 132-133)

Objectives
Students will:
- use context clues to help determine the meaning of the word that fits the context.

Summary of Lesson Material
Coupon clippers have an annual convention where they exchange information about saving. These collectors are very organized.

Teaching Suggestions
In **Lesson 2,** point out that several of the new words can be either nouns or verbs *(interchange, approach, register, proceeds)*. Ask students which part of speech applies in the reading context. You might also bring out the meaning of *inter* ("between") and ask students to name additional *inter* words. In addition, have volunteers look up *circulation* in a dictionary and explain how its meaning is related to that of *circular.*

Answer Key
A. **1.** b, **2.** b, **3.** a, **4.** a, **5.** b, **6.** b, **7.** a, **8.** b
B. **1.** interchange, **2.** proceeds, **3.** pursuit, **4.** contend
C. Answers will vary.

LESSON 3 ☐ Moviemaking in Cities (Pages 134-135)

Objectives
Students will:
- use context clues to help determine the meaning of the word that fits the context.

Summary of Lesson Material
Filmmakers are finding it cheaper and more interesting to film directly in city streets. Cities are benefitting from the notoriety and money.

Teaching Suggestions
When introducing the new vocabulary in **Lesson 3,** ask students if they know two ways to pronounce *content.* Ask which pronunciation is correct in the

selection. Also, make sure students don't confuse *content* with *contend* from the previous lesson. Ask students which two words are movie terms *(features, extras)*, and have them look for additional movie terms in the selection. Explain that *premier* is a homonym of the movie term *premiere*, but the words have different meanings. Also point out that other words in the selection have multiple meanings. Have students use a dictionary to find at least two meanings for *inviting, cast, capital, centers, sets,* and *commercial*.

In reviewing the answers to the exercises, have students explain which context clues helped them arrive at the correct answers.

Answer Key
A. 1. b, **2.** a, **3.** b, **4.** b, **5.** a, **6.** b, **7.** a, **8.** b, **9.** a, **10.** a
B. 1. commission, **2.** colorful, **3.** assurance, **4.** dictated
C. Answers will vary.

WORD REVIEW (Page 136)

Objectives
Students will:
- review ten of the new words from the previous three lessons.

Summary of Lesson Material
Students use new words to replace synonyms in ten sentences.

Teaching Suggestions
Encourage students to actually rewrite the sentences to reinforce their ability to use the new words.

Review answers aloud after students have completed the exercise. As an additional activity, students may make up their own sentences using other lesson words. Or students may write sentences illustrating different meanings of the same words.

Answer Key
1. flexible, **2.** ascent, **3.** ultimate, **4.** contend, **5.** pursuit, **6.** interchange,
7. eclipse, **8.** commission, **9.** feature, **10.** assurance

TAKING TESTS (Page 137)

Objectives
Students will:
- become familiar with another testing format.
- show mastery of the vocabulary words and skills covered in the previous three lessons.

Summary of Lesson Material
Students will identify which usage of a multiple-meaning word in a sentence matches a given definition. Eight definitions are given, each followed by three choices.

Teaching Suggestions
Review the **Test Tips** and read the directions with students. Make sure they understand where to locate the definition they are to match. If students are using answer sheets to record their answers (see pages 83-96 of this Manual), tell them to fill in the space on the answer sheet that corresponds with the item number and answer choice letter. Point out that students will not fill in the entire grid.

After students have completed the test, review the answers together. Note which words gave the students particular difficulty, and review using context clues as a way to choose the best answer. Note also that the definitions presented in items 7 and 8 are different from those that fit in the lessons themselves.

Answer Key
1. b, **2.** a, **3.** b, **4.** c, **5.** c, **6.** b, **7.** a, **8.** b

EXTENSION ACTIVITIES

The following are suggested activites to reinforce and enrich students' skills in using multiple-meaning words:

1. Have students work in pairs, Give each pair a list of 10 multiple-meaning words. Using a dictionary, each pair must write two sentences illustrating two different meanings of each of the 10 words. The first pair to write all 20 sentences correctly wins.

2. In Lesson 3, students discussed special movie-related meanings of common words. Have students pick other subject areas and list common words with special meanings in the subject area. (For example: What are the special law-related meanings of *book, brief, conviction, offense,* and *suite?)*

3. Have each student write a sentence that uses a multiple-meaning word in two different ways. (For example: I *contend* that it is wrong for two friends to *contend* for the same job.) Have students read the sentence aloud, saying "blank" in place of the word. Let classmates try to guess the missing word.

PART 4 □ WORD PARTS

Introduction (Pages 138-141)

Objectives
Students will:
- focus on identification of word parts as an aid to determining the meaning of a new word.
- will look for the base word in order to infer the meaning of the new word.

Summary of Lesson Material
Page 138 shows two pictures to which the students are to match the words *ablaze* and *disorderly.* Pages 139-141 presents common prefixes and suffixes that are added to base words and three exercises typical of this part of the vocabulary unit.

Teaching Suggestions
Pages 138-141 present explanation and self-checking practice exercises. Work through the exercises with students. Have students identify the base word they find within each new word. Discuss how the meaning of the new word is

related to the meaning of the base word. Call attention to the different prefixes and suffixes defined on page 139. Discuss how these beginnings and endings affect the meaning of a base word.

Answer Key
Page 139: 1. a, **2.** b, **3.** b
Page 140-141: A. 1. c, **2.** e, **3.** b, **4.** a, **5.** d
B. 1. frightful, **2.** recreate, **3.** outskirts, **4.** demonic, **5.** prehistoric
C. 1. b, **2.** c, **3.** a, **4.** c, **5.** c

LESSON 1 ☐ Baseball's Mystery Mud (Pages 142-143)

Objectives
Students will:
- identify word parts as an aid to determining the meaning of a new word.
- look for the base word in order to infer the meaning of the new word.

Summary of Lesson Material
Major league baseballs are covered with a special mud called "Lena Blackburne's Baseball Rubbing Mud". This mud, applied by the homeplate umpire, makes the balls less shiny and slippery.

Teaching Suggestions
In this lesson, have students look for words they know in the lesson words. Ask them to identify the compound word (*safeguard*). Also, have students identify the new words that contain the prefixes or suffixes they reviewed earlier (*pre: precedes; over: overcautious; under: undersupplied: re: restock; ive: secretive; ify: notify; ous: overcautious*).

Answer Key
A. 1. b, **2.** a, **3.** a, **4.** c, **5.** b, **6.** b, **7.** a, **8.** c
B. Answers will vary.

LESSON 2 ☐ Connecting the Generations (Pages 144-145)

Objectives
Students will:
- focus on identification of word parts as an aid to determining the meaning of a new word.
- look for the base word in order to infer the meaning of the new word.

Summary of Lesson Material
Kathy Levin started "Magic Me" in Baltimore, MD. This program recruits students to become volunteers in nursing homes and hospitals.

Teaching Suggestions
When introducing the new vocabulary in **Lesson 2,** ask students which words deal with thoughts or feelings (*underestimate, desirous, knowledgeable, sensitive, repress*). Also ask students to identify the compound word on the list (*breakthrough*). Then call attention to the prefixes and suffixes used in many of the lesson words. Have students identify as many as they can. Ask them to point out the base words and to note how the words are used in the reading selection.

In each lesson, after students have completed exercise A, review the answers together. As additional practice in exercise B, have students write questions and answers using the other lesson words.

Answer Key
A. 1. b, **2.** a, **3.** a, **4.** c, **5.** b, **6.** a, **7.** a, **8.** c
B. Answers will vary.

TAKING TESTS (Page 146)

Objectives
Students will:
■ become familiar with another vocabulary testing technique.
■ show mastery of the vocabulary words and skills covered in the last two lessons.

Summary of Lesson Material
Students will infer the meaning of a word based on its word parts and its context in a sentence. Eight sentences are given.

Teaching Suggestions
Review the directions and **Test Tips** with students. If they are using answer sheets to record their answers (see pages 83-96 of this Manual), tell students to fill in the space on the answer sheet that corresponds with the item humber and answer choice letter. Point out that students will not fill in the entire grid.

After students have completed the test, review answers with them. Note which items presented difficulty, and review accordingly.

Answer Key
1. b, **2.** c, **3.** a, **4.** d, **5.** c, **6.** c, **7.** b, **8.** d

EXTENSION ACTIVITIES

The following are suggested activities to reinforce and enrich students' skills in recognizing and using word parts.

1. Give students a common base word, such as *claim*. Have them make as many words as possible from the base word. (For example: *claimant, proclaim, reclaim, disclaim, declaim, exclaim.*)

2. If you think your students are ready, give them a list of common Latin or Greek roots, such as *post, duc, loc, spect, manu*. Have them write out groups of English words that contain each root, and then explain how the meaning of each word is related to the root's meaning.

GLOSSARY (Pages 218-220)

A Glossary containing all the lesson words in the **Vocabulary Unit** is presented at the end of the student book. It may be used to help students check their answers to the vocabulary exercises or as a review.

Suggest that students cover the definitions with an index card and try to give the correct meaning for a word. Perhaps classmates can call out the words (or definitions) while students give the definitions (or words).

As an additional activity, have students look in a dictionary to find other meanings for the Glossary words.

UNIT III *Study Skills*

PART 1 □ VISUAL MATERIAL

Introduction (Pages 148-149)

Objectives
Students will:
- be presented three basic types of visual material: maps, tables, and graphs.
- be shown the techniques for getting information from each type of material.

Summary of Lesson Material
A passage about Third World countries is followed by a world map showing these countries, a table of their borrowing powe, a graph showing percent of money these countries have borrowed from the World Bank, and four multiple choice questions.

Teaching Suggestions
The map, table, and graph introduce the type of visual materials presented in Part 1 of this unit. Discuss students' previous experience with maps, tables, and graphs.

After students have completed the questions, have volunteers explain the answers.

Answer Key
1. d, **2.** b, **3.** c, **4.** a

LESSON 1 □ Inner Space (Pages 150-151)
READING A ROAD MAP

Objectives
Students will:
- use a map scale and a compass rose to determine the distance and direction between two locations on a road map.
- use a map key to determine which highway to travel between two locations.

Summary of Lesson Material
A selection about Carlsbad Caverns in New Mexico is followed by a road map of the area and eight questions.

Teaching Suggestions
The first four lessons in this section deal with map reading. Point out to students that while they may be familiar with road maps, there are many other kinds of maps, such as product maps, special-purpose maps, and contour maps. This part of the unit will introduce students to a variety of maps.

Before students begin answering the questions, call attention to the map scale, compass rose, and map key. Have volunteers explain the purpose of each of these features. Explain that all maps are not drawn to the same proportion, so it is impossible to determine distances without the map scale provided for each particular map. Encourage students to use a ruler when figuring the distance between two locations.

Review all answers with students. Let volunteers explain how they used the compass rose, map key, or map scale to arrive at each answer.

Answer Key
1. c, **2.** b, **3.** c, **4.** c, **5.** b, **6.** a, **7.** a, **8.** c

LESSON 2 ☐ Salting It Away (Pages 152-153)
READING A SPECIAL-PURPOSE MAP

Objectives
Students will:
■ use a special-purpose map to determine average salaries for residents of some states in the United States.

Summary of Lesson Material
A passage about the origin of the word salary is followed by an economic map of the central states of the United States showing average salares.

Teaching Suggestions
Point out that this type of map is far different from a road map, since a special-purpose map requires no use of a compass rose or map scale. Call attention, however, to the need for a map key, which is essential in interpreting the symbols that signify different income amounts.

   Explain that the information shown on this map might also have been presented in a chart or table. Discuss why a map might be a more useful way of presenting average incomes across the country. Mention that by using a map, students may more easily compares incomes of states in one particular area such as in the Midwest or the South.

Answer Key
1. d, **2.** c, **3.** a, **4.** c, **5.** c, **6.** b, **7.** b, **8.** d

LESSON 3 ☐ The Terrific Tree of Tenerife (Pages 154-155)
READING A CONTOUR MAP

Objectives
Students will:
■ use a map key to interpret information on a contour map.
■ determine elevations of various locations on Tenerife Island.

Summary of Lesson Material
The "dragon tree", a treelike plant that grows on the Canary Islands, is described in a short passage followed by a contour map of Tenerife Island.

Teaching Suggestions
Make sure students understand that the measurements on this type of map are not distances between two locations, but rather measurements of heights. As with a road map and special-purpose map, the map key is essential in interpreting information on a contour map. However, a map scale is not necessary to determine elevations.

   Discuss with students how a contour map might be useful to a mountain climber or surveyor. Remind students that the measurements on this particular map are shown in meters. One meter equals 39.37 inches, or a little more than three feet. A kilometer is 1,000 meters or 3,281 feet.

Answer Key
1. a, **2.** c, **3.** d, **4.** c, **5.** b, **6.** c, **7.** c, **8.** a

LESSON 4 ☐ Sources of Resources (Pages 156-157)
GETTING INFORMATION FROM MAPS

Objectives
Students will:
- obtain information from product maps.
- read and interpret product maps of Australia and India.

Summary of Lesson Material
Students will identify which areas produce particular minerals, and will identify minerals mined in one country but not in the other after reading a short selection about the earth's mineral distribution and studying mineral product maps of Australia and India.

Teaching Suggestions
Have a volunteer explain the necessity of a map key in understanding a product map. In reviewing answers, have a volunteer explain why a map scale was not necessary in answering any of the questions.

Answer Key
1. a, **2.** c, **3.** c, **4.** a, **5.** b, **6.** d, **7.** , **8.** a, **9.** b

LESSON 5 ☐ In Peace and War (Pages 158-159)
READING A TABLE

Objectives
Students will:
- use a table to obtain information.

Summary of Lesson Material
A brief selection about the enlistment of men and women in the Armed Forces is followed by a table of enlistments over a forty year period. Students will use the table to determine the number of people enlisted in the U.S. Army and Navy in specific years between 1940 and 1980.

Teaching Suggestions
Point out to students that reading is in two directions—from left to right and from top to bottom. The table in this lesson has two columns, so students must be extra careful when reading down to make sure they use the correct column.

When reviewing answers, have volunteers explain how they derived each answer choice. Discuss which mathematical procedures were needed to answer items 4, 5, 7, and 8.

Answer Key
1. a, **2.** c, **3.** c, **4.** a, **5.** b, **6.** d, **7.** a, **8.** b

LESSON 6 ☐ Women and the Changing Job Market (Pages 160-161)
READING A LINE GRAPH

Objectives
Students will:
- use a graph to obtain specific information.

Summary of Lesson Material
A graph of work areas where women have gained employment in recent years

is presented. Students will determine the percentage of female workers in five job categories.

Teaching Suggestions
Explain to students that a graph is similar to a table because it is read in two directions—across and down. A line graph best shows how something increases or decreases over a period of time. The line graph in this lesson, where more than one line appears on the grid, is actually a complex line graph. Caution students to read the correct line when answering questions. Also caution students about reading the correct year on the graph for each question.

Answer Key
1. c, 2. c, 3. a, 4. a, 5. c, 6. b, 7. d, 8. d

LESSON 7 ☐ Train Travel (Pages 162-163)
READING A BAR GRAPH

Objectives
Students will:
- use a bar graph to obtain information.

Summary of Lesson Material
A bar graph representing the number of railroad cars sold in a specific year is presented. Students determine the number of railcars sold in given years.

Teaching Suggestions
Explain that a bar graph can be used to vividly depict the differences between two or more items. Have students study the information shown in the bar graph in this lesson. Ask whether or not the information could also have been displayed on a line graph.

Discuss which type of graph students think would be most effective in presenting the information about sales of railcars. When reviewing answers, have students explain how addition and subtraction were necessary to answer items 5 and 6.

Answer Key
1. d, 2. a, 3. c, 4. a, 5. b, 6. a, 7. b, 8. c

LESSON 8 ☐ Voting Patterns (Pages 164-165)
READING A COMPLEX BAR GRAPH

Objectives
Students will:
- use a complex bar graph to get information.

Summary of Lesson Material
Students will determine the percentage of voters in different age categories who voted in two different elections. This information is obtained from the selection and complex bar graph presented on page 164.

Teaching Suggestions

Remind students that a bar graph is used to compare two or more different things. A complex bar graph is a combination of two or more bar graphs that appear on the same grid. Discuss the way the different age brackets are depicted by the different bars. Also emphasize the importance of referring to the correct bar when searching for specific information to answer a question.

Answer Key

1. b, **2.** a, **3.** c, **4.** c, **5.** b, **6.** d, **7.** c, **8.** a

LESSON 9 ☐ Keeping the Faith (Pages 166-167)
READING CIRCLE GRAPHS

Objectives

Students will:

■ use circle graphs to determine information.

Summary of Lesson Material

Students compare two circle graphs to determine the percentages of church members of several faiths in the United States and in the world.

Teaching Suggestions

Explain that a circle graph is used to show percentages, or parts of a whole. The percentages in a circle graph add up to 100%. Each section in a graph appears in proportion to the amount it represents. For example, 25% on a circle graph would take up ¼ of the space within the circle. Caution students to use the correct graph when answering questions.

Answer Key

1. a, **2.** b, **3.** c, **4.** b, **5.** b, **6.** c, **7.** c, **8.** d

LESSON 10 ☐ The United Nations: A Matter of Opinion (Pages 168-169)
GETTING INFORMATION FROM GRAPHS AND TABLES

Objectives

Students will:

■ use a bar graph and a table to get facts.

Summary of Lesson Material

A bar graph showing U.N. membership and a table showing Americans' attitudes toward that organization for a thirty-year period are presented. Students will use these visual materials to get facts about the growth of the United Nations, and its standing in public opinion.

Teaching Suggestions

The two kinds of visual materials give different information; students must decide which resource to use to answer each question. When reviewing answers, have a volunteer explain why both the table and the graph are necessary to answer item 8.

Answer Key

1. a, **2.** c, **3.** c, **4.** a, **5.** c, **6.** d, **7.** a, **8.** a

TAKING TESTS (Pages 170-173)

Objectives
Students will:
■ show mastery of the skills taught in the previous ten lessons by applying their knowledge of reading and interpreting maps, tables, charts, and graphs.

Summary of Test Material (Pages 170-171)
A road map, a bar graph, a complex bar graph and a complex line graph are presented; each is preceded by a test tip and followed by three multiple choice questions.

Summary of Test Material (Pages 172-173)
A circle graph and a chart about a presidential election are presented followed by three multiple choice questions. A chart and a rainfall map are included, each followed by three multiple choice questions. The tests end with four general questions regarding visual materials.

Teaching Suggestions
Review the directions and the **Test Tips** with the students before they begin each test. If students are using answer sheets to record their answers (see pages 83-96 of this Manual), tell them to fill in the space on the answer sheet that goes with the letter of the answer they choose. To change an answer, they must erase the old mark completely and make a new mark.

After students have completed the tests, you may wish to review the answers aloud. Note where students may have had difficulty working with a particular visual material, and then review those skills.

Answer Key
Page 170: 1. a, **2.** a, **3.** c, **4.** b, **5.** c, **6.** c
Page 171: 7. a, **8.** a, **9.** c, **10.** b, **11.** b, **12.** b
Page 172: 13. c, **14.** b, **15.** c, **16.** a, **17.** b, **18.** a
Page 173: 19. a, **20.** b, **21.** c, **22.** b, **23.** a, **24.** c, **25.** b

EXTENSION ACTIVITIES

The following are suggested activities to reinforce and enrich students' skills in using visual materials:

1. Have students draw a road map showing a route between their home and school, or two other locations of their choice. The maps should include symbols or significant places found within the area depicted: parks, important buildings, rivers, bridges, etc. Have students provide a map key to explain each symbol.

2. Suggest that students collect data on how they spend their leisure time: sports activities, reading, TV, movies, telephone conversations, etc. They can then present the information in the form of a bar graph.

3. Students can take a survey among themselves to determine the kind of music they like best—classical, rock'n'roll, jazz, country and western, etc. After conversation into percentages, the information can be displayed on a circle graph.

PART 2 □ REFERENCE SKILLS

Introduction (Pages 174-175)

Objectives
Students will:
- be introduced to basic reference sources: dictionaries, encyclopedias, atlases, almanacs, newspapers, and magazines.
- use a table of contents, and index, the card catalog, and the *Readers' Guide to Periodical Literature.*

Summary of Lesson Material
Beekeeping as a hobby is discussed on page 175. It is followed by a picture representation of reference material in which more information on the subject could be obtained.

Teaching Suggestions
As in Part 1 of this unit, the first item in each lesson is self-checking. Discuss students' familiarity with the reference sources shown on pages 174-175. Have students tell when and where they have used any of these sources.

After students have answered the questions, review their answers orally. If possible, have each reference material available so that students may study the contents of each.

Answer Key
1. d, **2.** b, **3.** d

LESSON 1 □ A Boom Is on the Way (Pages 176-177)
USING A DICTIONARY

Objectives
Students will:
- be introduced to the basic features of a dictionary.
- use guide words to locate the page on which entry words may be found.
- identify the number of syllables, the part of speech, and the various meanings for an entry word.

Summary of Lesson Material
According to computer predictions from analysis of the 1980 census, there will be a population boom, or growth, in the rural mountain states in the U.S. The dictionary page on which growth can be found is pictured.

Teaching Suggestions
Begin the lesson by asking students what information they can find in a dictionary. Besides mentioning a word's meaning or spelling, students may mention pronunciation or etymology (history). Inform students that many dictionaries also have special features in the back such as listings of biographical names, geographical names, or foreign words and phrases.

After students read through the material on page 176 and the top of 177, have them complete the exercise on page 177. Note that items 4 and 7 require making an inference. When reviewing answers, have volunteers explain how they chose their answers for those particular items.

Answer Key
1. d, **2.** b, **3.** b, **4.** d, **5.** a, **6.** a, **7.** c, **8.** c

LESSON 2 □ Bacteria Aren't *All* Bad (Pages 178-179)
USING A TABLE OF CONTENTS AND AN INDEX

Objectives
Students will:
- locate information in a book.
- use chapter titles to infer the contents of chapters.
- use titles and cross references in an index to identify the pages on which specific information can be found.

Summary of Lesson Material
Positive information about bacteria and illustrations of a table of contents and an index where more information on bacteria can be found are presented.

Teaching Suggestions
Begin the lesson by asking students what types of books usually have a table of contents. Most textbooks or other nonfiction books, which may be divided by chapters or units, usually have a table of contents. Discuss that the usefulness of such table gives the reader a quick overview of the information to be found in the book. The same applies to an index. Point out that an index lists its topics alphabetially, while a table of contents lists its titles chronologically.

Answer Key
1. a, **2.** b, **3.** c, **4.** b, **5.** c, **6.** b, **7.** d, **8.** d

LESSON 3 □ Welcome Home, Computers (Pages 180-181)
USING THE CARD CATALOG

Objectives
Students will:
- learn to locate library books and find information about them.
- identify the type of card (title, author, or subject) necessary to locate a particular book, given specific information about the book.
- identify the date of publication and the call number for books listed in the card catalog.

Summary of Lesson Material
Information about uses of home computers can be listed in three different ways on catalog cards. Examples are shown.

Teaching Suggestions
Explain that title cards are arranged alphabetically according to the first important word in the title. (For example: The First Olympics would be listed under "F", not "T".) Also explain that author cards are arranged alphabetically by last name. (For example, a book by Henry Johnson would be listed under "J," not "H".)

Answer Key
1. c, **2.** d, **3.** c, **4.** b, **5.** c, **6.** d, **7.** a, **8.** a

LESSON 4 ☐ Swimming Anyone? (Pages 182-183)
USING THE *READERS' GUIDE TO PERIODICAL LITERATURE*

Objectives
Students will:
- learn to find magazine articles on specific subjects.
- identify which magazine contains a particular article.
- identify the author, title, page number, and publication date of the article.

Summary of Lesson Material
Swimming is the topic that is used to illustrate the use of *Readers' Guide to Periodical Literature*.

Teaching Suggestions
Remind students that a card catalog lists library books, but not magazines. Students may think of the *Readers' Guide* as a card catalog for magazines. Like the card catalog, the *Readers' Guide* lists the title, subject and author for each article. You may wish to review the abbreviations used for months, as well as those used for magazines, such as for *Sports Illustrated*. Inform students that they can find an explanation for all abbreviations at the beginning of each volume of the *Readers' Guide*.

Answer Key
1. a, **2.** c, **3.** d, **4.** c, **5.** c, **6.** d, **7.** b, **8.** c

LESSON 5 ☐ Uncovering the Past (Pages 184-185)
USING AN ENCYCLOPEDIA

Objectives
Students will:
- identify which volume of a multivolume encyclopedia to use to locate specific information.
- use an encyclopedia index and the guide letters on the spine of each voluem to locate the information.

Summary of Lesson Material
Some information about the history of Vesuvius is given and more information is available in the encyclopedia, as the illustrations and exercises show.

Teaching Suggestions
Ask students on what occasions they have used an encyclopedia. Discuss the types of information and articles it contains. Explain that an encyclopedia has an index similar to a textbook index. It lists topics alphabetically to help the reader locate specific information. Explain to students that when using the index, they should look under the more general topic before looking for a specific subtopic. For example, in searching for information about John Kennedy's inauguration, students would first look under "Kennedy," and then look in that article for information about the Kennedy inauguration.

Answer Key
1. a, **2.** d, **3.** c, **4.** b, **5.** c, **6.** b, **7.** a, **8.** b

LESSON 6 □ An Unexpected Meeting (Pages 186-187)
USING AN ATLAS

Objectives
Students will:
- use an atlas index to identify the page numbers and map coordinates for specific locations.

Summary of Lesson Material
A passage about the recent discovery of a primitive tribe in Burma is followed by a map of Burma and a section of an atlas index showing Burma.

Teaching Suggestions
Explain to students that an atlas is a book of maps. Although students may find maps in encyclopedias, it is often easier to locate a map in an atlas, which is a more complete collection. Point out that many atlases give the populations of the areas listed. When working with the lesson, make sure students understand how to use map coordinates. Explain that it involves running one finger down the page and another finger across the page simultaneously to the point designated by the map coordinates. Remind students that one feature found on a map is a compass rose, which students will need to answer item 5. Review all answers orally.

Answer Key
1. b, 2. c, 3. b, 4. d, 5. c, 6. c, 7. c, 8. d

LESSON 7 □ Brooklyn Babies (Pages 188-189)
USING AN ALMANAC

Objectives
Students will:
- determine the pages on which specific information would be found in an almanac by using its index.
- get information from an almanac listing.

Summary of Lesson Material
Two excerpts from an almanac are shown following a passage about the number of entertainers who have come from Brooklyn.

Teaching Suggestions
Explain to students that an almanac, like an encyclopedia, has an index to help the reader locate information. An almanac index is used similarly to an encyclopedia. Students would look under the more general topic before looking for a more specific subtopic. (For example, to find information about expenditures of the Department of Energy, students would look first under "Energy, Dept. of," and then under "expenditures.") Ask students when they might find an almanac more useful than an encyclopedia. Point out that both resources contain information on the same topics, but an almanac, published annually, is more up-to-date. When using an almanac index, students should note the cross references, which may help them locate even more information about a topic.

Answer Key
1. c, 2. b, 3. d, 4. d, 5. c, 6. b, 7. a, 8. d

LESSON 8 □ Money, Money, Money (Pages 190-191)
USING NEWSPAPER AND MAGAZINES

Objectives
Students will:
- read selections from both a newspaper and a magazine.
- identify whether a newspaper or magazine would be the better source to use for specific information.

Summary of Lesson Material
A newspaper article and a magazine article about the value of money are compared.

Teaching Suggestions
Start the lesson by asking students which magazines or newspapers they read fairly regularly. Discuss the type of information found in each source. Ask students what differences they might find between an article in a magazine and one in a newspaper that covered the same topic. Point out that a newspaper contains the most up-to-date information a reader can get, since it is usually printed daily. A magazine article, on the other hand, must be written at least a few days before distribution, so news may not be as current. Still, it is more current than information in an almanac or encyclopedia. When answers are reviewed, have volunteers explain how they arrived at each answer choice.

Answer Key
1. d, **2.** b, **3.** c, **4.** a, **5.** b, **6.** a, **7.** a, **8.** b

LESSON 9 □ Daybreak Debate (Pages 192-193)
CHOOSING THE RIGHT REFERENCE

Objectives
Students will:
- review the following reference sources: dictionaries, encyclopedias, atlases, almanacs, newspapers, the card catalog, and *Readers' Guide.*
- identify which reference to use to locate specific information.

Summary of Lesson Material
Facts about the "Sunrise County" of the U.S.A. are presented and their sources discussed.

Teaching Suggestions
Have volunteers name all the reference sources they can think of. Let them list the type of information to be found in each one. Students may chart this information to keep as a handy reference. Then read through the introductory paragraphs on page 192. Discuss which sources might have been used to gather the information in the passage.

 After students have completed the exercises, review all the answers orally. Have volunteers explain their answer choices.

Answer Key
1. b, **2.** d, **3.** a, **4.** c, **5.** b, **6.** a, **7.** c, **8.** d

TAKING TESTS (Pages 194-196)

Objectives
Students will:
- show mastery of the reference skills taught in the previous nine lessons by applying their knowledge of finding information in the reference material.

Summary of Taking Tests (Pages 194-195)
Presents four **Test Tips** about reference skills, each followed by multiple choice questions.

Summary of Taking Tests (Pages 196)
Ten questions about the purpose of each type of reference material are presented.

Teaching Suggestions
Review the directions and **Test Tips** with the students before they begin each test. If students are using answer sheets to record their answers (see pages 83-96 of this Manual), tell them to fill in the space on the answer sheet that goes with the letter of the answer they choose.

   After students have completed each test, review the answers orally. Note any difficulty students had with particular reference sources, and review accordingly.

Answer Key
Page 194: 1. c, **2.** c, **3.** b, **4.** c, **5.** b, **6.** a, **7.** c
Page 195: 8. c, **9.** c, **10.** b, **11.** c, **12.** b, **13.** d
Page 196: 14. c, **15.** b, **16.** d, **17.** d, **18.** b, **19.** d, **20.** a, **21.** b, **22.** c, **23.** a

EXTENSION ACTIVITIES

The following are suggested activities to reinforce and enrich students' skills in using reference materials:

1. Have students organize a class card catalog. Three cards—for title, subject, author—should be made out for each book they have recently read. Cards can be added as more books are read throughout the year.

2. Suggest that students choose a subject of interest to them and look up specific information in appropriate sources. For example, the subject may be baseball. Information to be found can include: the history of the game *(encyclopedia);* the winners of last year's World Series *(almanac);* the name of the pitchers in last night's game *(newspaper);* a profile of a prominent player *(magazine);* a compilation of dictionary terms *(dictionary);* the location of cities with major league teams *(atlas).* Similar exercises can be adapted for films, space launchings, or other subjects or events.

(Pages 197-217)

Objectives
Students will:
- show mastery of all the skills covered in the book.
- improve their reading and test-taking skills.
- become familiar with the format of achievement tests.

Summary of Tests
Two complete tests are presented. Each one has three sections: **Reading Comprehension, Vocabulary,** and **Study Skills.** The Reading Comprehension section requires students to find details and main ideas, make inferences, and determine the author's purpose in reading selections. The Vocabulary section requires students to determine word meanings by recognizing synonyms, antonyms, context clues, multiple-meaning words, and word parts. (Note that in the multiple-meaning section, students may work with a meaning that was not necessarily the meaning used in the lesson. This way, students practice the skill of applying various meanings of a word, based on its sentence context.) The Study Skills section requires students to read information on maps, tables, and graphs, and to identify and locate information found in different reference sources.

Teaching Suggestions
Review the directions with the students at the beginning of each test section, or have students read the directions on their own. You may review the **Test Tips** that accompany the tests within each unit. Also review with students the method of recording answers on the answer sheets (see pages 83-96 of this Manual).

Since a major purpose of the tests is to prepare students for timed achievement tests they will take in school, yo may wish to set a time limit for each test. The following is a suggested guideline:

TEST 1
Reading Comprehension—20 minutes
Vocabulary—8 minutes
Study Skills—22 minutes

Test 2
Reading Comprehension—18 minutes
Vocabulary—6 minutes
Study Skills—22 minutes

ANSWER KEY—TEST 1

Reading Comprehension (pages 198-201)
1. c, **2.** a, **3.** d, **4.** b, **5.** d, **6.** c, **7.** a, **8.** b,
9. c, **10.** b, **11.** c, **12.** d, **13.** b, **14.** c, **15.** b,
16. d, **17.** c, **18.** b

Vocabulary (pages 202-204)
1. d, **2.** c, **3.** a, **4.** c, **5.** b, **6.** d, **7.** b, **8.** d,
9. c, **10.** b, **11.** c, **12.** a, **13.** b, **14.** d, **15.** c,
16. a, **17.** d, **18.** a, **19.** a, **20.** d, **21.** c, **22.** b,
23. c, **24.** a, **25.** a, **26.** c, **27.** b, **28.** a

Study Skills (pages 205-207)
1. c, **2.** a, **3.** b, **4.** b, **5.** c, **6.** b, **7.** c, **8.** a,
9. c, **10.** b, **11.** a, **12.** c, **13.** a, **14.** c, **15.** c,
16. a, **17.** d, **18.** a, **19.** c, **20.** b, **21.** d, **22.** c,
23. a, **24.** d, **25.** b

ANSWER KEY—TEST 2

Reading Comprehension (pages 208-211)
1. c, **2.** a, **3.** c, **4.** d, **5.** a, **6.** c, **7.** c, **8.** d,
9. c, **10.** d, **11.** b, **12.** a, **13.** c, **14.** c, **15.** b,
16. a, **17.** d

Vocabulary (pages 212-214)
1. c, **2.** b, **3.** d, **4.** a, **5.** b, **6.** d, **7.** b, **8.** d,
9. a, **10.** d, **11.** b, **12.** c, **13.** d, **14.** a, **15.** c,
16. b, **17.** a, **18.** c, **19.** d, **20.** b, **21.** c, **22.** a,
23. b, **24.** d, **25.** c, **26.** b

Study Skills (pages 215-217)
1. a, **2.** c, **3.** b, **4.** d, **5.** c, **6.** b, **7.** d, **8.** c,
9. b, **10.** c, **11.** b, **12.** a, **13.** c, **14.** a, **15.** c,
16. d, **17.** b, **18.** a, **19.** d, **20.** c, **21.** b, **22.** c,
23. b, **24.** d, **25.** a

Printmaster Sheets

Carefully read each passage and the questions that follow. In the Answer Box below, fill in the circled letter for the correct choice.

On September 4, 1986, Prince Charles, the future King of England, attended a convocation at Harvard University. The Prince was invited to help Harvard celebrate its 350th birthday by delivering the Foundation Day Speech. He told the crowd of 16,000 students and scholars gathered for the ceremonies, that it was the largest audience he had addressed since speaking to 40,000 Gujerati buffalo farmers in India in 1980.

Prince Charles graduated from Cambridge University in England. Cambridge was the school from which John Harvard (the founder of Harvard University) graduated. Many Harvard graduates thought that this connection was not enough reason for a foreign prince to speak at an American university, especially in Boston, birthplace of the American Revolution.

The heir to the British throne spoke about the importance of Anglo-American ties. He also stated that modern education should teach values as well as knowledge. Everything went so well that no one seemed to miss the elegant Princess Di.

1. A good title for this passage might be _____ .
   a. Harvard's Birthday
   b. Anglo-American Relations
   c. A Princely Visit
   d. 350 Years at Harvard

2. The founder of Harvard University was _____ .
   a. Prince Charles
   b. John Harvard
   c. Anglo-America
   d. none of the above

3. The word *convocation* in this selection means _____ .
   a. a celebration
   b. a graduation ceremony
   c. a gathering or assembly
   d. a summons to appear before a group

4. Prince Charles was welcomed to Harvard _____ .
   a. reluctantly by some
   b. by the Board of Trustees
   c. enthusiastically by all
   d. only by the students

5. Prince Charles believes that modern education should _____ .
   a. be abolished
   b. go back to the basics
   c. guarantee that all people go to college
   d. teach values as well as knowledge

Answer Box

1. (a) (b) (c) (d)
2. (a) (b) (c) (d)
3. (a) (b) (c) (d)
4. (a) (b) (c) (d)
5. (a) (b) (c) (d)

If you've been watching TV commercials lately, you may be confused. Commercials are designed to make you want to buy something, but today, you really don't know what you're supposed to buy.

This trend, or direction in advertising, started with Coca Cola and Pepsi Cola. Their manufacturers believed that the public was eager to buy these products. All the advertisers had to do, then, was to remind the public that the products were there. Since then, however, TV ad campaigns have become increasingly confusing.

Commercials for denim jeans have gone so far as to completely ignore the product. Calvin Klein originated this presentation a few years ago. He had his models talk about anything but jeans. Of course, they were wearing "Calvins" as they talked. Jordache followed this lead. In some Jordache commercials, teenagers talk about everything from acne to their first attempts at romance. They never mention the jeans. The idea behind the ad is to focus attention on the conversation of "real" teenagers. Young people then make the connection between hip dialogue and the jeans the hip models are wearing. The message is that to be hip or "real," you must wear Jordache jeans.

Networks have refused to air some of these commercials. Parents and women's groups have accused ad agencies of encouraging youngsters to speak and behave inappropriately. They are hoping that like all fads, this form of advertising will eventually end.

6. TV commercials are becoming confusing because _____ .
   a. networks have refused to air some of them
   b. you don't know what products are being sold
   c. there are too many actors in them
   d. they are not produced in color

7. Another word for **trend** in this selection is _____ .
   a. commercial   c. direction
   b. advertisement   d. agency

8. The commercials that completely ignore their products are frequently selling _____ .
   a. cosmetics   c. denim jeans
   b. Pepsi Cola   d. Coca Cola

9. The first manufacturer to ignore the product in commercials was _____ .
   a. Jordache   c. Pepsi
   b. Coke   d. Calvin Klein

10. Ads for jeans sell the product by _____ .
   a. encouraging viewers to relate to the dialogue
   b. relying on viewers to admire the actors
   c. emphasizing the quality of the product
   d. making the product look interesting and attractive

Answer Box

6. (a) (b) (c) (d)
7. (a) (b) (c) (d)
8. (a) (b) (c) (d)
9. (a) (b) (c) (d)
10. (a) (b) (c) (d)

Carefully read each passage and the questions that follow.

Tetherball or Punch Ball is a game that can be played by young and old. All you need is a pole, a ball and some rope. You can buy a complete set or make your own. The pole, sunk 8 inches below the ground, should extend 10 feet above ground level. The ball and rope are attached to the pole. The ball hangs 2 feet above the ground. The court is a circle 20 feet in diameter with the pole in the middle. The court is divided in half with each player assigned to his half.

Rules

Fouls: **1.** Hitting the ball with any part of the body other than the hands or forearms.
2. Stopping continuous play by holding or catching the ball.
3. Touching the pole with any part of the body.
4. Interfering with the progress of the game by hitting the rope.
5. Playing the ball while standing outside a player's area.

Penalty: A player who commits a foul listed above forfeits the game to the opponent. Play stops immediately after a foul.

Scoring: The game is won by the player who first winds the rope completely around the pole. A player can also win by forfeit if a foul has been committed.

Choose the best answer for each question. In the Answer Box below, fill in the circled letter for the correct answer choice.

1. Tetherball is played on _____ .
   a. grass
   b. a rectangular area
   c. a circular court
   d. a square court

2. A player must avoid _____ .
   a. committing a foul
   b. touching the ball with the hands
   c. hitting the pole with the ball
   d. standing inside a player's area

3. The game is won when _____ .
   a. the ball is wrapped around the pole
   b. a player earns 21 points
   c. a foul is committed
   d. a and c only

4. The total length of the Tetherball pole is _____ .
   a. 10 feet, 10 inches
   b. 8 feet
   c. 12 feet, 8 inches
   d. 10 feet, 8 inches

5. When hitting the ball, a player can _____ .
   a. use any part of the body
   b. use hands and forearms only
   c. use only one foot
   d. use either the head or the feet

Answer Box
1. (a) (b) (c) (d)
2. (a) (b) (c) (d)
3. (a) (b) (c) (d)
4. (a) (b) (c) (d)
5. (a) (b) (c) (d)

Many Americans were either amused or upset when Secretary of State William Seward purchased Alaska from Russia in 1867. The cost of the purchase was seven million dollars. What did America get? Millions of acres of land covered with ice and snow. For years people called Alaska "Seward's Folly" and "Seward's Icebox."

Thirty years later in June 1897 the steamship *Excelsior* sailed from Juneau, Alaska and docked in San Francisco. Little attention was paid to its unshaven group of passengers. But word soon got around as the passengers began to unpack their luggage. Their bundles and battered boxes contained gold! The news flashed from coast to coast. Gold had been found on the Klondike River in Alaska!

A gold rush was on. Men from all over the world hurried to the northern gold fields. Claims were staked on every creek in the area. The first winter was grim. Many men starved or were frozen to death. But with the spring thaws came gold, and those who could work found themselves rich.

In recent years Alaska has seen another gold rush, this one for "black gold." Pools of oil were found just under the frozen surface. Today, the Alaskan pipeline pumps its wealth down to the "lower 48."

Americans have discovered the wild, untamed beauty of the Alaskan wilderness. Each year thousands of Americans travel to our northernmost state to enjoy the clean air, beautiful mountains, friendly native people, and wild animals running free.

Alaska, which became the 49th state in 1959, was hardly "Seward's Folly". It is a proud state that has added its beauty and wealth to a grateful America.

Choose the best answer for each question. In the Answer Box below, fill in the circled letter for the correct choice.

6. Gold was discovered in Alaska in _____ .
   a. 1849
   b. 1867
   c. 1897
   d. 1959

7. Alaska was purchased _____ .
   a. from the Alaskan natives
   b. in 1867 from Russia
   c. in 1897 from Canada
   d. by President Seward for $6,000,000

8. The phrases "black gold" and "lower 48" refer to _____ .
   a. gold nuggets and the northwestern states
   b. oil and the United States
   c. mountains and valleys
   d. rich soil and Mexico

9. The first ship that carried the news of gold in Alaska was the _____ .
   a. *Seward's Folly*   c. *Seward's Icebox*
   b. *Excelsior*   d. *Golden Eagle*

10. Alaksa became the 49th American state in _____ .
    a. 1960   c. 1959
    b. 1949   d. 1869

Answer Box

6. (a) (b) (c) (d)
7. (a) (b) (c) (d)
8. (a) (b) (c) (d)
9. (a) (b) (c) (d)
10. (a) (b) (c) (d)

Comprehension Post Test 2 Answers: 6. c 7. b 8. b 9. b 10. c

Carefully read each passage and the questions that follow.

A trip to the dentist can be a horrifying experience. The main reason for this is the dentist's drill. However, if a new technique proves to be successful, the whir (and pain) of the drill may be a thing of the past.

The new technique uses warm, salty water which acts as a mild acid. The acid is pumped into a tooth that needs filling. As the decayed area is painlessly softened, the dentist rubs off the decay and fills the cavity. This method is so painless, one study reports, that 90% of the patients didn't need an anesthetic.

This new method, called Caridex, has been tested for ten years. Dentists have found that patients suffered no side effects from it. By the end of 1986, approximately 1/5 of America's dentists will know how to use this new procedure. The next time you hear a dentist say, "This won't hurt a bit," he may be right.

Choose the best answer for each question. In the Answer Box below, fill in the circled letter for the correct choice.

1. The Caridex technique may eventually eliminate _____ .
   a. filling teeth   c. cleaning teeth
   b. scraping tarter   d. drilling cavities

2. The Caridex technique uses _____ .
   a. mild acid to arrest decay
   b. salt water as a softening agent
   c. acid as a cleanser
   d. regular water to prevent decay

3. The Caridex technique has been _____ .
   a. used successfully by many dentists
   b. tested for 10 years
   c. approved by the government
   d. used by 30% of American dentists

4. The word *anesthetic* is used in this passage to mean _____ .
   a. pain
   b. treatment
   c. pain killer
   d. drilling

5. A good title for this article might be _____ .
   a. "Painless Dentistry at Last"
   b. "Acid Dissolves Decay"
   c. "The End of Tooth Decay"
   d. "No Need to Brush"

Answer Box

1. (a) (b) (c) (d)
2. (a) (b) (c) (d)
3. (a) (b) (c) (d)
4. (a) (b) (c) (d)
5. (a) (b) (c) (d)

Has your room ever been referred to as "a disaster area" because it's littered with clothing? Recently, some theories have been proposed as to why teenagers don't use closets as storage facilities for clothes.

One theory, or explanation of why things happen, is that teenager's don't hang their clothes up because they think that clothes hangers are radioactive. These teens are convinced that if they touch a hanger, they will be severely burned. One young man insisted that clothes hangers were filled with germs. He believed that a person could become very sick by wearing clothes which had been in contact with a hanger.

Another theory is that teenagers are convinced that their beds should be used for more than sleeping. One sixteen-year-old girl said that the area under the bed was really designed as a hamper to store clothes over a long period of time. She said that, in fact, some of her clothes had been stored under her bed for almost sixteen months.

Still another theory says that teenagers believe that closets are off limits to them. These young men and women say that closets are never opened by anyone under twenty-one years old. Many of them even argued that an anti-closet law has been on the books for years.

Experts do not see any hope for parents of teenagers. They do not think that parents will ever convince their children to hang up their clothes.

But parents are not giving up. One father has reportedly designed a vacuum that sucks clothes from under beds right into a washing machine. Another parent is said to have invented a hanger which beeps until you hang a garment on it. The only problem is that no one can hear the beep. There are too many clothes piled on top of the hanger.

Choose the best answer for each question.

6. The author of this passage is _____ .
   a. someone who dislikes teenagers
   b. a neat freak
   c. taking an amused attitude towards teenagers
   d. a closet salesman

7. According to the passage, some teenagers believe that closets _____ .
   a. are off limits to them
   b. can be radioactive
   c. are really hampers
   d. should always be neat

8. What is a theory?
   a. an interview with a psychologist
   b. an explanation of why something happens
   c. a feeling about clothes
   d. the reason for an illness

9. One teenager mentioned in the passage believes that _____ .
   a. beds were made for sleeping
   b. closet doors should be left open
   c. clothes hangers are covered with germs
   d. every bedroom needs a hamper

10. How is one desperate parent dealing with clothes on the floor?
   a. by having teenagers arrested.
   b. by calling doctors for help.
   c. by taking the doors off of closets.
   d. by inventing things to clean up the rooms.

Answer Box

6. (a) (b) (c) (d)
7. (a) (b) (c) (d)
8. (a) (b) (c) (d)
9. (a) (b) (c) (d)
10. (a) (b) (c) (d)

Vocabulary PRETEST 1

Choose the correct meaning of the word in dark type in each sentence. In the Answer Box below, fill in the circled letter for the correct choice.

1. **discontinued** service
   a. enhanced
   b. halted
   c. competitive
   d. repeated

2. **factual** story
   a. silly
   b. easy
   c. true
   d. difficult

3. **expedite** matters
   a. solidify
   b. difficult
   c. accelerate
   d. glowing

4. **grueling** race
   a. easy
   b. specific
   c. exterior
   d. hard

5. **impaired** hearing
   a. injured
   b. good
   c. perfect
   d. doubled

6. **relinquished** ownership
   a. gave up
   b. holding
   c. perfect
   d. final

7. a **knowledgeable** person
   a. well-known
   b. informed
   c. uninformed
   d. invisible

8. **flexible** bandage
   a. permanent
   b. worn
   c. bendable
   d. strong

9. **optimistic** person
   a. lost
   b. foreign
   c. found
   d. hopeful

10. **revered** scientist
    a. respected
    b. known
    c. nuclear
    d. shunned

Answer Box

1.	ⓐ	ⓑ	ⓒ	ⓓ	6.	ⓐ	ⓑ	ⓒ ⓓ
2.	ⓐ	ⓑ	ⓒ	ⓓ	7.	ⓐ	ⓑ	ⓒ ⓓ
3.	ⓐ	ⓑ	ⓒ	ⓓ	8.	ⓐ	ⓑ	ⓒ ⓓ
4.	ⓐ	ⓑ	ⓒ	ⓓ	9.	ⓐ	ⓑ	ⓒ ⓓ
5.	ⓐ	ⓑ	ⓒ	ⓓ	10.	ⓐ	ⓑ	ⓒ ⓓ

Choose the word or phrase that best completes each sentence. Fill in the correct letter in the Answer Box below.

1. If your supplies are **dwindling,** your supplies are _____ .
   a. increasing
   b. being stolen
   c. decreasing
   d. being resupplied

2. **Incarcerated** people are _____ .
   a. imprisoned
   b. capable of working
   c. injured
   d. freed

3. A **valiant** person is _____ .
   a. insecure
   b. brave
   c. flexible
   d. unusual

4. If you **abet** criminals, you _____ .
   a. underestimate them
   b. comply with them
   c. hinder them
   d. aid them

5. An **enlightened** person is _____ .
   a. boastful
   b. bashful
   c. wise
   d. unconcerned

6. If you **expunge** a mistake, you _____ .
   a. change it
   b. emphasize it
   c. erase it
   d. forget it

7. A **petroleum** company sells _____ .
   a. oil
   b. glass
   c. coal
   d. pets

8. A **fictional** story is a story _____ .
   a. based on fact
   b. that is long and boring
   c. about history
   d. that is made up

9. **Pragmatic** people are _____ .
   a. lazy
   b. busy
   c. practical
   d. inquisitive

10. To **repress** information is to _____ .
    a. give it freely
    b. hold it back
    c. disregard it
    d. analyze it

Answer Box

1. ⓐ	ⓑ	ⓒ	ⓓ	6. ⓐ	ⓑ	ⓒ	ⓓ
2. ⓐ	ⓑ	ⓒ	ⓓ	7. ⓐ	ⓑ	ⓒ	ⓓ
3. ⓐ	ⓑ	ⓒ	ⓓ	8. ⓐ	ⓑ	ⓒ	ⓓ
4. ⓐ	ⓑ	ⓒ	ⓓ	9. ⓐ	ⓑ	ⓒ	ⓓ
5. ⓐ	ⓑ	ⓒ	ⓓ	10. ⓐ	ⓑ	ⓒ	ⓓ

Vocabulary

A. Read the incomplete sentence carefully. Decide which word you are being asked to define in the sentence. This is the key word. Look for the answer choice that is a synonym of the key word.

1. If you are **shunned,** you _____ .
   a. understand it
   b. are welcomed
   c. are avoided
   d. exposed to it

2. To be a **statesman** is to be _____ .
   a. a candidate for political office
   b. a governor of a state
   c. President
   d. all of the above

3. If you draw an **arch,** you draw _____ .
   a. a straight line   c. a circle
   b. a curve   d. a square

4. If you have a **dialogue** with someone, you _____ .
   a. walk with them
   b. dance with them
   c. disagree with them
   d. talk to them

5. If you **enroll** in something, you _____ .
   a. leave your job
   b. eat a buttered roll
   c. sign off
   d. sign up

B. Choose a word that means the opposite of the word in dark type in each item below. In the Answer Box below, mark the circled letter for the correct choice.

6. a **turbulent** ocean
   a. rough
   b. calm
   c. stormy
   d. wild

7. an **elaborate** program
   a. easily understood
   b. complicated
   c. hidden
   d. complex

8. an **implausible** situation
   a. brilliant
   b. complex
   c. unknown
   d. believable

9. a **renowned** person
   a. unknown
   b. noted
   c. famous
   d. not alive

10. a **glamorous** job
    a. fascinating
    b. hard
    c. long and complicated
    d. dull, boring

Answer Box

1. (a) (b) (c) (d)	6. (a) (b) (c) (d)
2. (a) (b) (c) (d)	7. (a) (b) (c) (d)
3. (a) (b) (c) (d)	8. (a) (b) (c) (d)
4. (a) (b) (c) (d)	9. (a) (b) (c) (d)
5. (a) (b) (c) (d)	10. (a) (b) (c) (d)

Vocabulary Post Test Answers:: 1. c, 2. d, 3. b, 4. d, 5. d, 6. b, 7. a, 8. d, 9. a, 10. d

Below the crossword puzzle is a list of definitions of words from the Glossary of your textbook. The vocabulary words themselves are the words to be placed in the puzzle.

ACROSS CLUES
1. ORDER
5. AID OR HELP
7. LEAVE
9. BENDABLE
10. PROBLEM OR EMERGENCY

DOWN CLUES
2. REDUCE OR LESSEN
3. DODGE OR ESCAPE
4. CHARACTERISTICS OR QUALITIES
6. APPROVE
8. REPAIR

WORD LIST

ABET	FLEXIBLE
CRISIS	RATIFY
CURTAIL	RECTIFY
DECREE	TRAITS
ELUDE	VACATE

Vocabulary MASTERY TEST 2

Look at the word in the dark type. Choose the word in the four choices below that is EITHER a synonym OR an antonym for the word in the dark type. In the Answer Box below, fill in the circled letter for the correct choice.

1. **impressive** show
   a. remarkable
   b. mundane
   c. canceled
   d. postponed

2. **ratify** the contract
   a. dictate
   b. approve
   c. cancel
   d. remove

3. **elude** the police
   a. join
   b. escape
   c. control
   d. mislead

4. **inhospitable** person
   a. kind
   b. happy
   c. overcautious
   d. desirous

5. **treacherous** path
   a. safe
   b. short
   c. long
   d. turbulent

6. **unoccupied** chair
   a. colored
   b. shunned
   c. nonexistent
   d. filled

7. **ultimate** praise
   a. fictional
   b. lowest
   c. inadequate
   d. notable

8. **singular** thought
   a. wholesome
   b. uncontrolled
   c. valiant
   d. passionate

9. **repress** a remark
   a. state
   b. hold back
   c. write
   d. interpret

10. **unified** group
    a. disjointed
    b. impressive
    c. well-known
    d. united

Answer Box

1. (a) (b) (c) (d)   6. (a) (b) (c) (d)
2. (a) (b) (c) (d)   7. (a) (b) (c) (d)
3. (a) (b) (c) (d)   8. (a) (b) (c) (d)
4. (a) (b) (c) (d)   9. (a) (b) (c) (d)
5. (a) (b) (c) (d)   10. (a) (b) (c) (d)

Use the graph to answer the first four questions. In the Answer Box below, fill in the letter for the correct answer.

1. According to the graph, since 1981 the teen labor force has _____ .
   a. dropped by 50 thousand
   b. risen
   c. stayed the same
   d. risen by 50 thousand

2. In both years cited, the number of teenagers who did not work numbered _____ .
   a. less than 1,000
   b. approximately 300,000
   c. no more than 200,000
   d. exactly 50,000

3. According to the graph, as the teenage population has gone down the rate of unemployment has _____ .
   a. risen
   b. stayed the same
   c. gone down
   d. the information to determine this is not given

4. A close reading of the graph tells you that _____ .
   a. more teenagers are working now than 5 years ago
   b. fewer teenagers were unemployed in 1981
   c. as the population of teenagers increases, the teenage unemployment level increases
   d. there has been a trend to greater teenage unemployment over the past 5 years

5. To see if there is a railroad station near your home, you would look _____ .
   a. at a map
   b. in a dictionary
   c. in a magazine
   d. at a bar graph

TEEN LABOR FORCE 1981, 1986

6. In which source would you look to see if a word could be used as both a noun and a verb?
   a. in the almanac   c. in an encyclopedia
   b. in a dictionary   d. in a table of contents

7. To find the day of the week on which your birthday falls next year, you would look _____ .
   a. in an encyclopedia   c. in an almanac
   b. at a calendar   d. in a dictionary

8. In which source would you look to find which continent has the highest mountain?
   a. *Readers' Guide*   c. a map
   b. an atlas   d. a dictionary

Answer Box

1. ⓐ ⓑ ⓒ ⓓ   6. ⓐ ⓑ ⓒ ⓓ
2. ⓐ ⓑ ⓒ ⓓ   7. ⓐ ⓑ ⓒ ⓓ
3. ⓐ ⓑ ⓒ ⓓ   8. ⓐ ⓑ ⓒ ⓓ
4. ⓐ ⓑ ⓒ ⓓ   9. ⓐ ⓑ ⓒ ⓓ
5. ⓐ ⓑ ⓒ ⓓ   10. ⓐ ⓑ ⓒ ⓓ

Use the graph below to answer the first four questions. In the Answer Box below, fill in the circled letter for the correct choice.

1. Drug arrests are currently _____ .
   a. lower than they were five years ago
   b. stabilized at 650,000 per year
   c. decreasing
   d. on the increase

2. The greatest rise in arrests occurred in the years _____ .
   a. 1970-1973   c. 1979-1982
   b. 1977-1979   d. 1983-1985

3. The greatest decline in arrests occurred in the years _____ .
   a. 1977-1979   c. 1974-1976
   b. 1979-1981   d. 1977-1978

4. In the fifteen year period covered by the graph, the number of arrests has _____ .
   a. fallen   c. doubled
   b. risen   d. tripled

5. In which source would you look for turnpikes that would take you from New York City to Chicago?
   a. the almanac   c. a dictionary
   b. a road atlas   d. an index

6. Which source would list the language from which a certain word is derived?
   a. an atlas   c. a newspaper
   b. a dictionary   d. an almanac

7. If you were looking for information on auto repair, you would look in _____ .
   a. the almanac   c. the card catalog
   b. *Readers' Guide* d. b and c

OFF THE STREETS
Number of arrests for drug violations, in thousands

Source: FBI Uniform Crime Reports

8. Where would you find an alphabetical list of articles in an encyclopedia
   a. the index
   b. the card catalog
   c. *Readers' Guide*
   d. the table of contents

9. To learn current sports scores and statistics, you would look in _____ .
   a. an encyclopedia   c. an almanac
   b. the card catalog   d. a newspaper

10. Which reference would be the least likely place to give information about vacation spots in your state?
    a. an atlas   c. an encyclopedia
    b. the almanac   d. the dictionary

Answer Box

1. (a) (b) (c) (d)   6. (a) (b) (c) (d)
2. (a) (b) (c) (d)   7. (a) (b) (c) (d)
3. (a) (b) (c) (d)   8. (a) (b) (c) (d)
4. (a) (b) (c) (d)   9. (a) (b) (c) (d)
5. (a) (b) (c) (d)   10. (a) (b) (c) (d)

Study Skills

Use the bar graph below to answer the first four questions. In the Answer Box below, fill in the answer space for your choice.

1. The only year in which Japan had a minus balance of trade was _____ .
   a. 1982   b. 1985   c. 1981   d. 1980

2. West Germany was ahead of Japan for _____ years.
   a. 3   b. 2   c. 1   d. 0

3. In 1985 West Germany was behind Japan by _____ .
   a. $25,000,000,000   c. $20,000,000
   b. $21,000   d. $22,000,000,000

4. In what year were the plus values of West Germany and Japan almost the same as the minus value of the U.S. in 1983?
   a. 1982   b. 1983   c. 1984   d. 1985

5. To learn the birthplace and year of birth for a famous actor, you would consult _____ .
   a. a dictionary
   b. the card catalog
   c. an encyclopedia index
   d. an almanac

6. To get up-to-date information about the stock market, you would consult _____ .
   a. an encyclopedia
   b. a newspaper
   c. an almanac
   d. a book on finance

7. To find a magazine article on science, you would consult _____ .
   a. the index of your science book
   b. the table of contents of your science book
   c. the card catalog
   d. *Readers' Guide*

OUT-OF-BALANCE TRADE BALANCES

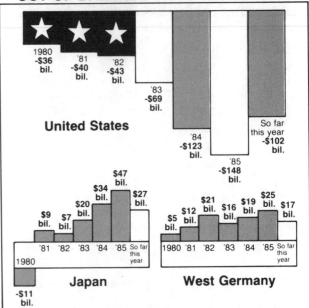

Note: 1986 figures are through July for U.S., through May for West Germany and Japan.
USN&WR—Basic data: U.S. Dept of Commerce, International Monetary Fund

8. If you were looking for specific information on forms of bacteria, you would look _____ .
   a. in the index of your science book
   b. in the table of contents of your science book
   c. in an almanac
   d. all of the above

9. To learn how to break a word into syllables, you would consult _____ .
   a. the card catalog   c. a dictionary
   b. a newspaper   d. an encyclopedia

10. To learn what countries are doing to combat terrorism at airports, you would consult _____ .
    a. a history book   c. an almanac
    b. an encyclopedia d. a magazine article

Answer Box

1. (a) (b) (c) (d)   6. (a) (b) (c) (d)
2. (a) (b) (c) (d)   7. (a) (b) (c) (d)
3. (a) (b) (c) (d)   8. (a) (b) (c) (d)
4. (a) (b) (c) (d)   9. (a) (b) (c) (d)
5. (a) (b) (c) (d) 10. (a) (b) (c) (d)

Read the Help Wanted Ads Below

LIFEGUARD

TRUMP PLAZA

HOTEL & CASINO
ON THE BOARDWALK

...currently has openings for

LIFEGUARDS

To qualify, you must be certified and possess at least 1 year related experience. Will be responsible for maintaining recreational facilities including, but not limited to swimming pools, shuffle board areas, and tennis courts.

We will offer attractive starting salaries and excellent benefits. Interested and qualified candidates should apply in person, Mon.-Fri. 9AM-4PM.

TRUMP PLAZA
EMPLOYMENT OFFICE

750 W. Delilah Road
Pleasantville, NJ 08232

For more information, call

(609) 484-7661

TRUMP PLAZA is an equal opportunity employer, subject to the rules and regulations of the NJ Casino Control Commission.

CLERKS

SECRETARIES

With and Without Steno

TYPISTS

DATA ENTRY

$50 BONUS

REGISTER AND FIND OUT ALL THE DETAILS. PLEASE, BRING THIS AD WITH YOU.

You name it-we have it! Our temporary assignments range from 1 day to 1 year. If you are serious about working-see us today and be on the job tomorrow earning top $$$. No fees. No contracts-just top assignments with the most prestigious corporations in Monmouth and Ocean counties. Vacation pay. Bonuses. Incentives. If you are registered with another agency, you can still work for us.

MANN

TEMPORARIES

43 Gilbert St., No.   Shrewsbury

842-4224

COLLECTION CLERK 50

COLLEGE STUDENT

EARN WHILE YOU LEARN, TELEPHONE CREDIT & COLLECTION CLERKS NEEDED NOW. HOURS ARE 5:30PM to 9PM, MON-THURS., 8AM-11PM SATURDAYS. LONG TERM. CO. LOCATED IN SHREWSBURY. GOOD HOURLY WAGE. DON'T WAIT. CALL FOR APPT.

MANPOWER, INC.
1 INDUSTRIAL WAY
EATONTOWN, N.J.

842-4343   542-5769

---

1. Which job would be the best for you?

2. Which job requires the least amount of education?

3. Which job requires the greatest amount of education?

4. Which job might require a driver's license?

5. Which job(s) require(s) a special skill?

6. Which job might require you to live away from home?

7. Which job might offer advancement?

WRITING EXERCISE

Below you will find a job application blank. Answer all questions fully and to the best of your ability. As you answer the questions, keep in mind that this application will be read by your future employer.

(PRE-EMPLOYMENT QUESTIONNAIRE)   (AN EQUAL OPPORTUNITY EMPLOYER)

Date_____

Name [Last Name First]_____ Soc. Sec. No._____

Address_____ Telephone_____

What kind of work are you applying for? _____

What special qualifications do you have _____

What office machines can you operate? _____

Are you 18 years or older?   Yes_____ No _____

SPECIAL PURPOSE QUESTIONS

DO NOT ANSWER **ANY** OF THE QUESTIONS IN THIS FRAMED AREA UNLESS THE EMPLOYER HAS **CHECKED A BOX PRECEDING** A QUESTION. THEREBY INDICATING THAT THE INFORMATION IS REQUIRED FOR A BONA FIDE OCCUPATIONAL QUALIFICATION, OR DICTATED BY NATIONAL SECURITY LAWS, OR IS NEEDED FOR OTHER LEGALLY PERMISSIBLE REASONS.

☐ HEIGHT_____ INCHES_____ ☐ WEIGHT_____LBS.   ☐ CITIZEN OF U.S.   YES_____ NO_____

☐ _____

MILITARY SERVICE RECORD

Armed Forces Service_____ Yes_____ No_____ From_____ To_____

Branch of Service_____ Duties _____

Rank or rating at time of enlistment_____ Rating at time of discharge _____

Do you have any physical limitations that prohibit you from performing any work for which you are being considered?   Yes_____ No_____ Please describe_____

EDUCATION

SCHOOL	*NO. OF YEARS ATTENDED	NAME OF SCHOOL	CITY	COURSE	*DID YOU GRADUATE?
GRAMMAR					
HIGH					
COLLEGE					
OTHER					

*The Age Discrimination in Employment Act of 1967 prohibits discrimination on the basis of age with respect to individuals who are at least 40 but less than 70 years of age.

EXPERIENCE

NAME AND ADDRESS OF COMPANY	DATE FROM	TO	LIST YOUR DUTIES	STARTING SALARY	FINAL SALARY	REASON FOR LEAVING

BUSINESS REFERENCES

NAME	ADDRESS	OCCUPATION

Answer Sheets

UNIT I Reading Comprehension Answer Sheet
Part 1 Details and Main Idea   Lessons 1-8 (pages 10-25)

1. (a) (b) (c) (d)   1. (a) (b) (c) (d)   1. (a) (b) (c) (d)   1. (a) (b) (c) (d)
2. (a) (b) (c) (d)   2. (a) (b) (c) (d)   2. (a) (b) (c) (d)   2. (a) (b) (c) (d)
3. (a) (b) (c) (d)   3. (a) (b) (c) (d)   3. (a) (b) (c) (d)   3. (a) (b) (c) (d)
4. (a) (b) (c) (d)   4. (a) (b) (c) (d)   4. (a) (b) (c) (d)   4. (a) (b) (c) (d)
5. (a) (b) (c) (d)   5. (a) (b) (c) (d)   5. (a) (b) (c) (d)   5. (a) (b) (c) (d)
6. (a) (b) (c) (d)   6. (a) (b) (c) (d)   6. (a) (b) (c) (d)   6. (a) (b) (c) (d)

1. (a) (b) (c) (d)   1. (a) (b) (c) (d)   1. (a) (b) (c) (d)   1. (a) (b) (c) (d)
2. (a) (b) (c) (d)   2. (a) (b) (c) (d)   2. (a) (b) (c) (d)   2. (a) (b) (c) (d)
3. (a) (b) (c) (d)   3. (a) (b) (c) (d)   3. (a) (b) (c) (d)   3. (a) (b) (c) (d)
4. (a) (b) (c) (d)   4. (a) (b) (c) (d)   4. (a) (b) (c) (d)   4. (a) (b) (c) (d)
5. (a) (b) (c) (d)   5. (a) (b) (c) (d)   5. (a) (b) (c) (d)   5. (a) (b) (c) (d)
6. (a) (b) (c) (d)   6. (a) (b) (c) (d)   6. (a) (b) (c) (d)   6. (a) (b) (c) (d)

Taking Tests (pages 26-29)

1. (a) (b) (c) (d)   6. (a) (b) (c) (d)   11. (a) (b) (c) (d)   16. (a) (b) (c) (d)
2. (a) (b) (c) (d)   7. (a) (b) (c) (d)   12. (a) (b) (c) (d)   17. (a) (b) (c) (d)
3. (a) (b) (c) (d)   8. (a) (b) (c) (d)   13. (a) (b) (c) (d)   18. (a) (b) (c) (d)
4. (a) (b) (c) (d)   9. (a) (b) (c) (d)   14. (a) (b) (c) (d)   19. (a) (b) (c) (d)
5. (a) (b) (c) (d)   10. (a) (b) (c) (d)   15. (a) (b) (c) (d)   20. (a) (b) (c) (d)

Part 2 Inference   Lessons 1-12 (pages 30-56)

1.   1. (a) (b) (c) (d)   2. (a) (b) (c) (d)   3. (a) (b) (c) (d)   4. (a) (b) (c) (d)
2.   1. (a) (b) (c) (d)   2. (a) (b) (c) (d)   3. (a) (b) (c) (d)   4. (a) (b) (c) (d)
3.   1. (a) (b) (c) (d)   2. (a) (b) (c) (d)   3. (a) (b) (c) (d)   4. (a) (b) (c) (d)
4.   1. (a) (b) (c) (d)   2. (a) (b) (c) (d)   3. (a) (b) (c) (d)   4. (a) (b) (c) (d)
5.   1. (a) (b) (c) (d)   2. (a) (b) (c) (d)   3. (a) (b) (c) (d)   4. (a) (b) (c) (d)
6.   1. (a) (b) (c) (d)   2. (a) (b) (c) (d)   3. (a) (b) (c) (d)   4. (a) (b) (c) (d)
7.   1. (a) (b) (c) (d)   2. (a) (b) (c) (d)   3. (a) (b) (c) (d)   4. (a) (b) (c) (d)
8.   1. (a) (b) (c) (d)   2. (a) (b) (c) (d)   3. (a) (b) (c) (d)   4. (a) (b) (c) (d)
9.   1. (a) (b) (c) (d)   2. (a) (b) (c) (d)   3. (a) (b) (c) (d)   4. (a) (b) (c) (d)
10. 1. (a) (b) (c) (d)   2. (a) (b) (c) (d)   3. (a) (b) (c) (d)   4. (a) (b) (c) (d)
11. 1. (a) (b) (c) (d)   2. (a) (b) (c) (d)   3. (a) (b) (c) (d)   4. (a) (b) (c) (d)
12. 1. (a) (b) (c) (d)   2. (a) (b) (c) (d)   3. (a) (b) (c) (d)   4. (a) (b) (c) (d)

1.	5. (a) (b) (c) (d)	6. (a) (b) (c) (d)	7. (a) (b) (c) (d)	8. (a) (b) (c) (d)
2.	5. (a) (b) (c) (d)	6. (a) (b) (c) (d)	7. (a) (b) (c) (d)	8. (a) (b) (c) (d)
3.	5. (a) (b) (c) (d)	6. (a) (b) (c) (d)	7. (a) (b) (c) (d)	8. (a) (b) (c) (d)
4.	5. (a) (b) (c) (d)	6. (a) (b) (c) (d)	7. (a) (b) (c) (d)	8. (a) (b) (c) (d)
5.	5. (a) (b) (c) (d)	6. (a) (b) (c) (d)	7. (a) (b) (c) (d)	8. (a) (b) (c) (d)
6.	5. (a) (b) (c) (d)	6. (a) (b) (c) (d)	7. (a) (b) (c) (d)	8. (a) (b) (c) (d)
7.	5. (a) (b) (c) (d)	6. (a) (b) (c) (d)	7. (a) (b) (c) (d)	8. (a) (b) (c) (d)
8.	5. (a) (b) (c) (d)	6. (a) (b) (c) (d)	7. (a) (b) (c) (d)	8. (a) (b) (c) (d)
9.	5. (a) (b) (c) (d)	6. (a) (b) (c) (d)	7. (a) (b) (c) (d)	8. (a) (b) (c) (d)
10.	5. (a) (b) (c) (d)	6. (a) (b) (c) (d)	7. (a) (b) (c) (d)	8. (a) (b) (c) (d)
11.	5. (a) (b) (c) (d)	6. (a) (b) (c) (d)	7. (a) (b) (c) (d)	8. (a) (b) (c) (d)
12.	5. (a) (b) (c) (d)	6. (a) (b) (c) (d)	7. (a) (b) (c) (d)	8. (a) (b) (c) (d)

Taking Tests (pages 57-59)

1. (a) (b) (c) (d)	6. (a) (b) (c) (d)	11. (a) (b) (c) (d)
2. (a) (b) (c) (d)	7. (a) (b) (c) (d)	12. (a) (b) (c) (d)
3. (a) (b) (c) (d)	8. (a) (b) (c) (d)	13. (a) (b) (c) (d)
4. (a) (b) (c) (d)	9. (a) (b) (c) (d)	14. (a) (b) (c) (d)
5. (a) (b) (c) (d)	10. (a) (b) (c) (d)	15. (a) (b) (c) (d)

Part 3 Critical Reading
Lessons 1-7 (pages 60-75)

1.	1. (a) (b) (c) (d)	2. (a) (b) (c) (d)	3. (a) (b) (c) (d)	4. (a) (b) (c) (d)
2.	1. (a) (b) (c) (d)	2. (a) (b) (c) (d)	3. (a) (b) (c) (d)	4. (a) (b) (c) (d)
3.	1. (a) (b) (c) (d)	2. (a) (b) (c) (d)	3. (a) (b) (c) (d)	4. (a) (b) (c) (d)
4.	1. (a) (b) (c) (d)	2. (a) (b) (c) (d)	3. (a) (b) (c) (d)	4. (a) (b) (c) (d)
5.	1. (a) (b) (c) (d)	2. (a) (b) (c) (d)	3. (a) (b) (c) (d)	4. (a) (b) (c) (d)
6.	1. (a) (b) (c) (d)	2. (a) (b) (c) (d)	3. (a) (b) (c) (d)	4. (a) (b) (c) (d)
7.	1. (a) (b) (c) (d)	2. (a) (b) (c) (d)	3. (a) (b) (c) (d)	4. (a) (b) (c) (d)
1.	5. (a) (b) (c) (d)	6. (a) (b) (c) (d)	7. (a) (b) (c) (d)	8. (a) (b) (c) (d)
2.	5. (a) (b) (c) (d)	6. (a) (b) (c) (d)	7. (a) (b) (c) (d)	8. (a) (b) (c) (d)
3.	5. (a) (b) (c) (d)	6. (a) (b) (c) (d)	7. (a) (b) (c) (d)	8. (a) (b) (c) (d)
4.	5. (a) (b) (c) (d)	6. (a) (b) (c) (d)	7. (a) (b) (c) (d)	8. (a) (b) (c) (d)
5.	5. (a) (b) (c) (d)	6. (a) (b) (c) (d)	7. (a) (b) (c) (d)	8. (a) (b) (c) (d)
6.	5. (a) (b) (c) (d)	6. (a) (b) (c) (d)	7. (a) (b) (c) (d)	8. (a) (b) (c) (d)
7.	5. (a) (b) (c) (d)	6. (a) (b) (c) (d)	7. (a) (b) (c) (d)	8. (a) (b) (c) (d)

Taking Tests (pages 76-78)

1. (a) (b) (c) (d)	5. (a) (b) (c) (d)	9. (a) (b) (c) (d)	13. (a) (b) (c) (d)
2. (a) (b) (c) (d)	6. (a) (b) (c) (d)	10. (a) (b) (c) (d)	
3. (a) (b) (c) (d)	7. (a) (b) (c) (d)	11. (a) (b) (c) (d)	
4. (a) (b) (c) (d)	8. (a) (b) (c) (d)	12. (a) (b) (c) (d)	

UNIT II Vocabulary Answer Sheet
Part I Synonyms and Antonyms   Lesson 1 (pages 84-85)

A. 1. _____
   2. _____
   3. _____
   4. _____
   5. _____
   6. _____
   7. _____
   8. _____

B.
| 1. (a) (b) (c) |
| 2. (a) (b) (c) |
| 3. (a) (b) (c) |
| 4. (a) (b) (c) |

C. 1. _____
   2. _____
   3. _____

Lesson 2 (pages 86-87)

A. 1. _____
   2. _____
   3. _____
   4. _____
   5. _____
   6. _____
   7. _____
   8. _____

B.
| 1. (a) (b) (c) |
| 2. (a) (b) (c) |
| 3. (a) (b) (c) |
| 4. (a) (b) (c) |

C. 1. _____
   2. _____
   3. _____

Lesson 3 (pages 88-89)

A. 1. _____
   2. _____
   3. _____
   4. _____
   5. _____
   6. _____
   7. _____
   8. _____

B.
| 1. (a) (b) (c) |
| 2. (a) (b) (c) |
| 3. (a) (b) (c) |
| 4. (a) (b) (c) |

C. 1. _____
   2. _____
   3. _____

Lesson 4 (pages 90-91)

A. 1. _____
  2. _____
  3. _____
  4. _____
  5. _____
  6. _____
  7. _____
  8. _____

B.
1. ⓐ ⓑ ⓒ
2. ⓐ ⓑ ⓒ
3. ⓐ ⓑ ⓒ
4. ⓐ ⓑ ⓒ

C. 1. _____
  2. _____
  3. _____

Lesson 5 (pages 92-94)

A. 1. _____
  2. _____
  3. _____
  4. _____
  5. _____
  6. _____
  7. _____
  8. _____

B.
1. ⓐ ⓑ ⓒ
2. ⓐ ⓑ ⓒ
3. ⓐ ⓑ ⓒ
4. ⓐ ⓑ ⓒ

C. 1. _____
  2. _____
  3. _____
  4. _____
  5. _____

Lesson 6 (pages 98-99)

A. 1. _____
  2. _____
  3. _____
  4. _____
  5. _____
  6. _____
  7. _____
  8. _____

B.
1. ⓐ ⓑ ⓒ
2. ⓐ ⓑ ⓒ
3. ⓐ ⓑ ⓒ
4. ⓐ ⓑ ⓒ

C. 1. _____
  2. _____
  3. _____

Lesson 7 (pages 100-101)

A.
1. _____
2. _____
3. _____
4. _____
5. _____
6. _____
7. _____
8. _____

B.
1. (a) (b) (c)
2. (a) (b) (c)
3. (a) (b) (c)
4. (a) (b) (c)

C.
1. _____
2. _____
3. _____

Lesson 8 (pages 102-104)

A.
1. _____
2. _____
3. _____
4. _____
5. _____
6. _____
7. _____
8. _____

B.
1. (a) (b) (c)
2. (a) (b) (c)
3. (a) (b) (c)
4. (a) (b) (c)
5. (a) (b) (c)
6. (a) (b) (c)

C.
1. _____
2. _____
3. _____

Taking Tests (pages 106-109)

1. (a) (b) (c) (d)   6. (a) (b) (c) (d)
2. (a) (b) (c) (d)   7. (a) (b) (c) (d)
3. (a) (b) (c) (d)   8. (a) (b) (c) (d)
4. (a) (b) (c) (d)   9. (a) (b) (c) (d)
5. (a) (b) (c) (d)   10. (a) (b) (c) (d)

11. (a) (b) (c) (d)   16. (a) (b) (c) (d)
12. (a) (b) (c) (d)   17. (a) (b) (c) (d)
13. (a) (b) (c) (d)   18. (a) (b) (c) (d)
14. (a) (b) (c) (d)   19. (a) (b) (c) (d)
15. (a) (b) (c) (d)   20. (a) (b) (c) (d)

21. (a) (b) (c) (d)   26. (a) (b) (c) (d)
22. (a) (b) (c) (d)   27. (a) (b) (c) (d)
23. (a) (b) (c) (d)   28. (a) (b) (c) (d)
24. (a) (b) (c) (d)   29. (a) (b) (c) (d)
25. (a) (b) (c) (d)   30. (a) (b) (c) (d)

31. (a) (b) (c) (d)   36. (a) (b) (c) (d)
32. (a) (b) (c) (d)   37. (a) (b) (c) (d)
33. (a) (b) (c) (d)   38. (a) (b) (c) (d)
34. (a) (b) (c) (d)   39. (a) (b) (c) (d)
35. (a) (b) (c) (d)   40. (a) (b) (c) (d)

Part II Context Clues
Lesson 1 (pages 114-115)

A.

1. (a) (b) (c)			5. (a) (b) (c)
2. (a) (b) (c)			6. (a) (b) (c)
3. (a) (b) (c)			7. (a) (b) (c)
4. (a) (b) (c)			8. (a) (b) (c)

B. 1. _____
2. _____
3. _____
4. _____
5. _____
6. _____
7. _____
8. _____

C. 1. _____
2. _____
3. _____

Lesson 2 (pages 116-117)

A.

1. (a) (b) (c)			5. (a) (b) (c)
2. (a) (b) (c)			6. (a) (b) (c)
3. (a) (b) (c)			7. (a) (b) (c)
4. (a) (b) (c)			8. (a) (b) (c)

B. 1. _____
2. _____
3. _____
4. _____
5. _____
6. _____
7. _____
8. _____

C. 1. _____
2. _____
3. _____

Lesson 3 (pages 118-119)

A.

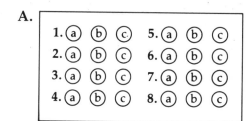

1. (a) (b) (c)			5. (a) (b) (c)
2. (a) (b) (c)			6. (a) (b) (c)
3. (a) (b) (c)			7. (a) (b) (c)
4. (a) (b) (c)			8. (a) (b) (c)

B. 1. _____
2. _____
3. _____
4. _____
5. _____
6. _____
7. _____
8. _____

C. 1. _____

   2. _____

   3. _____

Lesson 4 (pages 120-121)

A.

1. ⓐ	ⓑ	ⓒ	ⓓ	5. ⓐ	ⓑ	ⓒ	ⓓ
2. ⓐ	ⓑ	ⓒ	ⓓ	6. ⓐ	ⓑ	ⓒ	ⓓ
3. ⓐ	ⓑ	ⓒ	ⓓ	7. ⓐ	ⓑ	ⓒ	ⓓ
4. ⓐ	ⓑ	ⓒ	ⓓ	8. ⓐ	ⓑ	ⓒ	ⓓ

B. 1. _____

    2. _____

    3. _____

    4. _____

    5. _____

    6. _____

    7. _____

    8. _____

C. 1. _____

   2. _____

   3. _____

Taking Tests (pages 123-125)

1. ⓐ	ⓑ	ⓒ	ⓓ	6. ⓐ	ⓑ	ⓒ	ⓓ
2. ⓐ	ⓑ	ⓒ	ⓓ	7. ⓐ	ⓑ	ⓒ	ⓓ
3. ⓐ	ⓑ	ⓒ	ⓓ	8. ⓐ	ⓑ	ⓒ	ⓓ
4. ⓐ	ⓑ	ⓒ	ⓓ	9. ⓐ	ⓑ	ⓒ	ⓓ
5. ⓐ	ⓑ	ⓒ	ⓓ	10. ⓐ	ⓑ	ⓒ	ⓓ

11. ⓐ	ⓑ	ⓒ	ⓓ	15. ⓐ	ⓑ	ⓒ	ⓓ
12. ⓐ	ⓑ	ⓒ	ⓓ	16. ⓐ	ⓑ	ⓒ	ⓓ
13. ⓐ	ⓑ	ⓒ	ⓓ	17. ⓐ	ⓑ	ⓒ	ⓓ
14. ⓐ	ⓑ	ⓒ	ⓓ	18. ⓐ	ⓑ	ⓒ	ⓓ

19. ⓐ	ⓑ	ⓒ	ⓓ	23. ⓐ	ⓑ	ⓒ	ⓓ
20. ⓐ	ⓑ	ⓒ	ⓓ	24. ⓐ	ⓑ	ⓒ	ⓓ
21. ⓐ	ⓑ	ⓒ	ⓓ	25. ⓐ	ⓑ	ⓒ	ⓓ
22. ⓐ	ⓑ	ⓒ	ⓓ	26. ⓐ	ⓑ	ⓒ	ⓓ

Part 3 Words with Several Meanings
Lesson 1 (pages 130-131)

A.

1. ⓐ	ⓑ	5. ⓐ	ⓑ
2. ⓐ	ⓑ	6. ⓐ	ⓑ
3. ⓐ	ⓑ	7. ⓐ	ⓑ
4. ⓐ	ⓑ	8. ⓐ	ⓑ

B. 1. jump _____

    2. curve _____

    3. belief _____

    4. bendable _____

C. 1. _____
   2. _____
   3. _____

Lesson 2 (pages 132-133)

A.
1. (a) (b)	5. (a) (b)
2. (a) (b)	6. (a) (b)
3. (a) (b)	7. (a) (b)
4. (a) (b)	8. (a) (b)

B. 1. exchange _____
   2. profits _____
   3. occupation _____
   4. assert _____

C. 1. _____
   2. _____
   3. _____

Lesson 3 (pages 134-135)

A.
1. (a) (b)	6. (a) (b)
2. (a) (b)	7. (a) (b)
3. (a) (b)	8. (a) (b)
4. (a) (b)	9. (a) (b)
5. (a) (b)	10. (a) (b)

B. 1. committee _____
   2. lively _____
   3. guarantee _____
   4. demanded _____

C. 1. _____
   2. _____
   3. _____

Taking Tests (page 137)

A.
1. (a) (b) (c)	5. (a) (b) (c)
2. (a) (b) (c)	6. (a) (b) (c)
3. (a) (b) (c)	7. (a) (b) (c)
4. (a) (b) (c)	8. (a) (b) (c)

Part IV Word Parts
Lesson 1 (pages 142-143)

A.
1. (a) (b) (c)	5. (a) (b) (c)
2. (a) (b) (c)	6. (a) (b) (c)
3. (a) (b) (c)	7. (a) (b) (c)
4. (a) (b) (c)	8. (a) (b) (c)

B. 1. _____
   _____
   2. _____
   _____
   3. _____
   _____

Lesson 2 (pages 144-145)

A.

1. ⓐ ⓑ ⓒ	5. ⓐ ⓑ ⓒ
2. ⓐ ⓑ ⓒ	6. ⓐ ⓑ ⓒ
3. ⓐ ⓑ ⓒ	7. ⓐ ⓑ ⓒ
4. ⓐ ⓑ ⓒ	8. ⓐ ⓑ ⓒ

B.

1. _____

2. _____

3. _____

Taking Tests (Page 146)

1. ⓐ ⓑ ⓒ ⓓ	3. ⓐ ⓑ ⓒ ⓓ	5. ⓐ ⓑ ⓒ ⓓ	7. ⓐ ⓑ ⓒ ⓓ
2. ⓐ ⓑ ⓒ ⓓ	4. ⓐ ⓑ ⓒ ⓓ	6. ⓐ ⓑ ⓒ ⓓ	8. ⓐ ⓑ ⓒ ⓓ

UNIT III Study Skills Answer Sheet   Part 1 Visual Materials

Lesson 1 (page 151)

1. ⓐ ⓑ ⓒ ⓓ	5. ⓐ ⓑ ⓒ ⓓ
2. ⓐ ⓑ ⓒ ⓓ	6. ⓐ ⓑ ⓒ ⓓ
3. ⓐ ⓑ ⓒ ⓓ	7. ⓐ ⓑ ⓒ ⓓ
4. ⓐ ⓑ ⓒ ⓓ	8. ⓐ ⓑ ⓒ ⓓ

Lesson 2 (page 153)

1. ⓐ ⓑ ⓒ ⓓ	5. ⓐ ⓑ ⓒ ⓓ
2. ⓐ ⓑ ⓒ ⓓ	6. ⓐ ⓑ ⓒ ⓓ
3. ⓐ ⓑ ⓒ ⓓ	7. ⓐ ⓑ ⓒ ⓓ
4. ⓐ ⓑ ⓒ ⓓ	8. ⓐ ⓑ ⓒ ⓓ

Lesson 3 (page 155)

1. ⓐ ⓑ ⓒ ⓓ	5. ⓐ ⓑ ⓒ ⓓ
2. ⓐ ⓑ ⓒ ⓓ	6. ⓐ ⓑ ⓒ ⓓ
3. ⓐ ⓑ ⓒ ⓓ	7. ⓐ ⓑ ⓒ ⓓ
4. ⓐ ⓑ ⓒ ⓓ	8. ⓐ ⓑ ⓒ ⓓ

Lesson 4 (page 157)

1. ⓐ ⓑ ⓒ ⓓ	5. ⓐ ⓑ ⓒ ⓓ
2. ⓐ ⓑ ⓒ ⓓ	6. ⓐ ⓑ ⓒ ⓓ
3. ⓐ ⓑ ⓒ ⓓ	7. ⓐ ⓑ ⓒ ⓓ
4. ⓐ ⓑ ⓒ ⓓ	8. ⓐ ⓑ ⓒ ⓓ

Lesson 5 (page 159)

1. ⓐ ⓑ ⓒ ⓓ	5. ⓐ ⓑ ⓒ ⓓ
2. ⓐ ⓑ ⓒ ⓓ	6. ⓐ ⓑ ⓒ ⓓ
3. ⓐ ⓑ ⓒ ⓓ	7. ⓐ ⓑ ⓒ ⓓ
4. ⓐ ⓑ ⓒ ⓓ	8. ⓐ ⓑ ⓒ ⓓ

Lesson 6 (page 161)

1. ⓐ ⓑ ⓒ ⓓ	5. ⓐ ⓑ ⓒ ⓓ
2. ⓐ ⓑ ⓒ ⓓ	6. ⓐ ⓑ ⓒ ⓓ
3. ⓐ ⓑ ⓒ ⓓ	7. ⓐ ⓑ ⓒ ⓓ
4. ⓐ ⓑ ⓒ ⓓ	8. ⓐ ⓑ ⓒ ⓓ

Lesson 7 (page 163)

1. ⓐ ⓑ ⓒ ⓓ	5. ⓐ ⓑ ⓒ ⓓ
2. ⓐ ⓑ ⓒ ⓓ	6. ⓐ ⓑ ⓒ ⓓ
3. ⓐ ⓑ ⓒ ⓓ	7. ⓐ ⓑ ⓒ ⓓ
4. ⓐ ⓑ ⓒ ⓓ	8. ⓐ ⓑ ⓒ ⓓ

Lesson 8 (page 165)

1. ⓐ ⓑ ⓒ ⓓ	5. ⓐ ⓑ ⓒ ⓓ
2. ⓐ ⓑ ⓒ ⓓ	6. ⓐ ⓑ ⓒ ⓓ
3. ⓐ ⓑ ⓒ ⓓ	7. ⓐ ⓑ ⓒ ⓓ
4. ⓐ ⓑ ⓒ ⓓ	8. ⓐ ⓑ ⓒ ⓓ

Lesson 9 (page 167)

1. ⓐ ⓑ ⓒ ⓓ	5. ⓐ ⓑ ⓒ ⓓ
2. ⓐ ⓑ ⓒ ⓓ	6. ⓐ ⓑ ⓒ ⓓ
3. ⓐ ⓑ ⓒ ⓓ	7. ⓐ ⓑ ⓒ ⓓ
4. ⓐ ⓑ ⓒ ⓓ	8. ⓐ ⓑ ⓒ ⓓ

Lesson 10 (page 169)

1. ⓐ ⓑ ⓒ ⓓ	5. ⓐ ⓑ ⓒ ⓓ
2. ⓐ ⓑ ⓒ ⓓ	6. ⓐ ⓑ ⓒ ⓓ
3. ⓐ ⓑ ⓒ ⓓ	7. ⓐ ⓑ ⓒ ⓓ
4. ⓐ ⓑ ⓒ ⓓ	8. ⓐ ⓑ ⓒ ⓓ

Taking Tests
(page 170)

1. (a) (b) (c) (d)
2. (a) (b) (c) (d)
3. (a) (b) (c) (d)
4. (a) (b) (c) (d)
5. (a) (b) (c) (d)
6. (a) (b) (c) (d)

(page 171)

7. (a) (b) (c) (d)
8. (a) (b) (c) (d)
9. (a) (b) (c) (d)
10. (a) (b) (c) (d)
11. (a) (b) (c) (d)
12. (a) (b) (c) (d)

(page 172)

13. (a) (b) (c) (d)
14. (a) (b) (c) (d)
15. (a) (b) (c) (d)
16. (a) (b) (c) (d)
17. (a) (b) (c) (d)
18. (a) (b) (c) (d)

(page 173)

19. (a) (b) (c) (d)
20. (a) (b) (c) (d)
21. (a) (b) (c) (d)
22. (a) (b) (c) (d)
23. (a) (b) (c) (d)
24. (a) (b) (c) (d)
25. (a) (b) (c) (d)

Part 2 Reference Skills

Lesson 1 (page 177)

1. (a) (b) (c) (d)   5. (a) (b) (c) (d)
2. (a) (b) (c) (d)   6. (a) (b) (c) (d)
3. (a) (b) (c) (d)   7. (a) (b) (c) (d)
4. (a) (b) (c) (d)   8. (a) (b) (c) (d)

Lesson 2 (page 179)

1. (a) (b) (c) (d)   5. (a) (b) (c) (d)
2. (a) (b) (c) (d)   6. (a) (b) (c) (d)
3. (a) (b) (c) (d)   7. (a) (b) (c) (d)
4. (a) (b) (c) (d)   8. (a) (b) (c) (d)

Lesson 3 (page 181)

1. (a) (b) (c) (d)   5. (a) (b) (c) (d)
2. (a) (b) (c) (d)   6. (a) (b) (c) (d)
3. (a) (b) (c) (d)   7. (a) (b) (c) (d)
4. (a) (b) (c) (d)   8. (a) (b) (c) (d)

Lesson 4 (page 183)

1. (a) (b) (c) (d)   5. (a) (b) (c) (d)
2. (a) (b) (c) (d)   6. (a) (b) (c) (d)
3. (a) (b) (c) (d)   7. (a) (b) (c) (d)
4. (a) (b) (c) (d)   8. (a) (b) (c) (d)

Lesson 5 (page 185)

1. (a) (b) (c) (d)   5. (a) (b) (c) (d)
2. (a) (b) (c) (d)   6. (a) (b) (c) (d)
3. (a) (b) (c) (d)   7. (a) (b) (c) (d)
4. (a) (b) (c) (d)   8. (a) (b) (c) (d)

Lesson 6 (page 187)

1. (a) (b) (c) (d)   5. (a) (b) (c) (d)
2. (a) (b) (c) (d)   6. (a) (b) (c) (d)
3. (a) (b) (c) (d)   7. (a) (b) (c) (d)
4. (a) (b) (c) (d)   8. (a) (b) (c) (d)

Lesson 7 (page 189)

1. (a) (b) (c) (d)   5. (a) (b) (c) (d)
2. (a) (b) (c) (d)   6. (a) (b) (c) (d)
3. (a) (b) (c) (d)   7. (a) (b) (c) (d)
4. (a) (b) (c) (d)   8. (a) (b) (c) (d)

Lesson 8 (page 191)

1. (a) (b) (c) (d)   5. (a) (b) (c) (d)
2. (a) (b) (c) (d)   6. (a) (b) (c) (d)
3. (a) (b) (c) (d)   7. (a) (b) (c) (d)
4. (a) (b) (c) (d)   8. (a) (b) (c) (d)

Lesson 9 (page 193)

1. (a) (b) (c) (d)   5. (a) (b) (c) (d)
2. (a) (b) (c) (d)   6. (a) (b) (c) (d)
3. (a) (b) (c) (d)   7. (a) (b) (c) (d)
4. (a) (b) (c) (d)   8. (a) (b) (c) (d)

Taking Tests (page 194)

	a	b	c	d		a	b	c	d
1.	ⓐ	ⓑ	ⓒ	ⓓ	5.	ⓐ	ⓑ	ⓒ	ⓓ
2.	ⓐ	ⓑ	ⓒ	ⓓ	6.	ⓐ	ⓑ	ⓒ	ⓓ
3.	ⓐ	ⓑ	ⓒ	ⓓ	7.	ⓐ	ⓑ	ⓒ	ⓓ
4.	ⓐ	ⓑ	ⓒ	ⓓ	8.	ⓐ	ⓑ	ⓒ	ⓓ

(page 195)

	a	b	c	d		a	b	c	d
8.	ⓐ	ⓑ	ⓒ	ⓓ	12.	ⓐ	ⓑ	ⓒ	ⓓ
9.	ⓐ	ⓑ	ⓒ	ⓓ	13.	ⓐ	ⓑ	ⓒ	ⓓ
10.	ⓐ	ⓑ	ⓒ	ⓓ					
11.	ⓐ	ⓑ	ⓒ	ⓓ					

(page 196)

	a	b	c	d		a	b	c	d
14.	ⓐ	ⓑ	ⓒ	ⓓ	19.	ⓐ	ⓑ	ⓒ	ⓓ
15.	ⓐ	ⓑ	ⓒ	ⓓ	20.	ⓐ	ⓑ	ⓒ	ⓓ
16.	ⓐ	ⓑ	ⓒ	ⓓ	21.	ⓐ	ⓑ	ⓒ	ⓓ
17.	ⓐ	ⓑ	ⓒ	ⓓ	22.	ⓐ	ⓑ	ⓒ	ⓓ
18.	ⓐ	ⓑ	ⓒ	ⓓ	23.	ⓐ	ⓑ	ⓒ	ⓓ

Unit IV Tests Answer Sheet
Test 1: Reading Comprehension
(pages 198-199)

	a	b	c	d		a	b	c	d
1.	ⓐ	ⓑ	ⓒ	ⓓ	6.	ⓐ	ⓑ	ⓒ	ⓓ
2.	ⓐ	ⓑ	ⓒ	ⓓ	7.	ⓐ	ⓑ	ⓒ	ⓓ
3.	ⓐ	ⓑ	ⓒ	ⓓ	8.	ⓐ	ⓑ	ⓒ	ⓓ
4.	ⓐ	ⓑ	ⓒ	ⓓ					
5.	ⓐ	ⓑ	ⓒ	ⓓ					

(pages 200-201)

	a	b	c	d		a	b	c	d
9.	ⓐ	ⓑ	ⓒ	ⓓ	14.	ⓐ	ⓑ	ⓒ	ⓓ
10.	ⓐ	ⓑ	ⓒ	ⓓ	15.	ⓐ	ⓑ	ⓒ	ⓓ
11.	ⓐ	ⓑ	ⓒ	ⓓ	16.	ⓐ	ⓑ	ⓒ	ⓓ
12.	ⓐ	ⓑ	ⓒ	ⓓ	17.	ⓐ	ⓑ	ⓒ	ⓓ
13.	ⓐ	ⓑ	ⓒ	ⓓ	18.	ⓐ	ⓑ	ⓒ	ⓓ

Test 1: Vocabulary (pages 202-204)

	a	b	c	d		a	b	c	d
1.	ⓐ	ⓑ	ⓒ	ⓓ	6.	ⓐ	ⓑ	ⓒ	ⓓ
2.	ⓐ	ⓑ	ⓒ	ⓓ	7.	ⓐ	ⓑ	ⓒ	ⓓ
3.	ⓐ	ⓑ	ⓒ	ⓓ	8.	ⓐ	ⓑ	ⓒ	ⓓ
4.	ⓐ	ⓑ	ⓒ	ⓓ	9.	ⓐ	ⓑ	ⓒ	ⓓ
5.	ⓐ	ⓑ	ⓒ	ⓓ	10.	ⓐ	ⓑ	ⓒ	ⓓ

	a	b	c	d		a	b	c	d
11.	ⓐ	ⓑ	ⓒ	ⓓ	16.	ⓐ	ⓑ	ⓒ	ⓓ
12.	ⓐ	ⓑ	ⓒ	ⓓ	17.	ⓐ	ⓑ	ⓒ	ⓓ
13.	ⓐ	ⓑ	ⓒ	ⓓ	18.	ⓐ	ⓑ	ⓒ	ⓓ
14.	ⓐ	ⓑ	ⓒ	ⓓ	19.	ⓐ	ⓑ	ⓒ	ⓓ
15.	ⓐ	ⓑ	ⓒ	ⓓ	20.	ⓐ	ⓑ	ⓒ	ⓓ

	a	b	c	d		a	b	c	d
21.	ⓐ	ⓑ	ⓒ	ⓓ	25.	ⓐ	ⓑ	ⓒ	ⓓ
22.	ⓐ	ⓑ	ⓒ	ⓓ	26.	ⓐ	ⓑ	ⓒ	ⓓ
23.	ⓐ	ⓑ	ⓒ	ⓓ	27.	ⓐ	ⓑ	ⓒ	ⓓ
24.	ⓐ	ⓑ	ⓒ	ⓓ	28.	ⓐ	ⓑ	ⓒ	ⓓ

Test 1: Study Skills (pages 205-207)

1. (a) (b) (c) (d)　5. (a) (b) (c) (d)
2. (a) (b) (c) (d)　6. (a) (b) (c) (d)
3. (a) (b) (c) (d)　7. (a) (b) (c) (d)
4. (a) (b) (c) (d)　8. (a) (b) (c) (d)

9. (a) (b) (c) (d)　13. (a) (b) (c) (d)
10. (a) (b) (c) (d)　14. (a) (b) (c) (d)
11. (a) (b) (c) (d)　15. (a) (b) (c) (d)
12. (a) (b) (c) (d)　16. (a) (b) (c) (d)

17. (a) (b) (c) (d)　20. (a) (b) (c) (d)　23. (a) (b) (c) (d)
18. (a) (b) (c) (d)　21. (a) (b) (c) (d)　24. (a) (b) (c) (d)
19. (a) (b) (c) (d)　22. (a) (b) (c) (d)　25. (a) (b) (c) (d)

Test 2: Reading Comprehension (pages 208-211)

1. (a) (b) (c) (d)
2. (a) (b) (c) (d)
3. (a) (b) (c) (d)
4. (a) (b) (c) (d)
5. (a) (b) (c) (d)

6. (a) (b) (c) (d)
7. (a) (b) (c) (d)
8. (a) (b) (c) (d)
9. (a) (b) (c) (d)

10. (a) (b) (c) (d)
11. (a) (b) (c) (d)
12. (a) (b) (c) (d)
13. (a) (b) (c) (d)

14. (a) (b) (c) (d)
15. (a) (b) (c) (d)
16. (a) (b) (c) (d)
17. (a) (b) (c) (d)

Test 2: Vocabulary (pages 212-214)

1. (a) (b) (c) (d)
2. (a) (b) (c) (d)
3. (a) (b) (c) (d)
4. (a) (b) (c) (d)
5. (a) (b) (c) (d)
6. (a) (b) (c) (d)
7. (a) (b) (c) (d)
8. (a) (b) (c) (d)
9. (a) (b) (c) (d)
10. (a) (b) (c) (d)

11. (a) (b) (c) (d)
12. (a) (b) (c) (d)
13. (a) (b) (c) (d)
14. (a) (b) (c) (d)
15. (a) (b) (c) (d)
16. (a) (b) (c) (d)
17. (a) (b) (c) (d)
18. (a) (b) (c) (d)
19. (a) (b) (c) (d)
20. (a) (b) (c) (d)

21. (a) (b) (c) (d)
22. (a) (b) (c) (d)
23. (a) (b) (c) (d)
24. (a) (b) (c) (d)
25. (a) (b) (c) (d)
26. (a) (b) (c) (d)

Test 2: Study Skills (pages 215-217)

1. (a)	(b)	(c)	(d)
2. (a)	(b)	(c)	(d)
3. (a)	(b)	(c)	(d)
4. (a)	(b)	(c)	(d)
5. (a)	(b)	(c)	(d)
6. (a)	(b)	(c)	(d)
7. (a)	(b)	(c)	(d)
8. (a)	(b)	(c)	(d)

9. (a)	(b)	(c)	(d)
10. (a)	(b)	(c)	(d)
11. (a)	(b)	(c)	(d)
12. (a)	(b)	(c)	(d)
13. (a)	(b)	(c)	(d)
14. (a)	(b)	(c)	(d)
15. (a)	(b)	(c)	(d)
16. (a)	(b)	(c)	(d)

17. (a)	(b)	(c)	(d)
18. (a)	(b)	(c)	(d)
19. (a)	(b)	(c)	(d)
20. (a)	(b)	(c)	(d)
21. (a)	(b)	(c)	(d)
22. (a)	(b)	(c)	(d)
23. (a)	(b)	(c)	(d)
24. (a)	(b)	(c)	(d)
25. (a)	(b)	(c)	(d)